· MUSEUM OF NATURAL HISTORY · UNIVERSITY OF MINNESOTA ·

BIRD PORTRAITS IN COLOR

TWO HUNDRED NINETY-FIVE NORTH AMERICAN SPECIES

TEXT BY

THOMAS S. ROBERTS, M.D.

REVISED BY

Walter J. Breckenridge

Dwain W. Warner

Robert W. Dickerman

ILLUSTRATED WITH NINETY-TWO COLOR PLATES BY
ALLAN BROOKS · GEORGE MIKSCH SUTTON
WALTER ALOIS WEBER · FRANCIS LEE JAQUES
WALTER JOHN BRECKENRIDGE · INCLUDING ONE
PLATE BY THE LATE LOUIS AGASSIZ FUERTES

THE UNIVERSITY OF MINNESOTA PRESS

MINNEAPOLIS

PRINTED AND LITHOGRAPHED IN THE UNITED STATES OF AMERICA
BY McGILL GRAPHIC ARTS CENTER
ST. PAUL, MINNESOTA
14

Library of Congress Catalog Card Number: 60-14288

PUBLISHED IN GREAT BRITAIN, INDIA, AND PAKISTAN BY THE OXFORD UNIVERSITY PRESS
LONDON, BOMBAY, AND KARACHI, AND IN CANADA BY THOMAS ALLEN, LTD., TORONTO

The University of Minnesota, through its Museum of Natural History and the University Press, gratefully acknowledges the assistance Kate Koon Bovey has contributed to this publication. The admiration that Mrs. Bovey and her husband, the late Charles C. Bovey, held for Dr. Roberts, both as a physician and as an ornithologist, prompted her desire and efforts to promote this revised edition of his BIRD PORTRAITS IN COLOR. *Her own love of nature has convinced her that bringing this book back into print will provide a source of enjoyment to many bird lovers. Her generous guaranty of the additional funds needed for the enterprise has enabled the University of Minnesota to realize her aims and its own.*

INTRODUCTION

Bird Portraits in Color was first issued in 1934 and reprinted in 1936. Its ninety-two color plates originally illustrated *The Birds of Minnesota,* a two-volume work published in 1932. When it went out of print, the *Portraits,* with new text limited to one page for each plate, was made available for students and bird lovers for whom the more comprehensive work was too bulky for field use or too detailed. It too went out of print, in 1944. The continued demand for the volume has been gratifying; in response to it this new edition is being issued.

Although the title of the original publication, *The Birds of Minnesota,* limited it to one state, the species represented cover in large measure those found in temperate North America east of the Rocky Mountains. The text for each plate gives general information of value throughout much of the range of the birds discussed. Statements on the ranges of the species have been rewritten for this new edition to correspond with the distributions given in the recent fifth edition (1957) of *Checklist of North American Birds,* published by the American Ornithologists' Union. All scientific and common names also follow this authoritative source.

A brief statement regarding the classification of birds may be of interest. Birds are classified into *orders, families, genera, species,* and *subspecies.* The major divisions, orders and families, depend upon fundamental, generalized, structural characters; the minor divisions, genera and species, upon more specialized, adaptive characters. Several species grouped in a genus, while differing among themselves, must have in common certain generic characters and must also possess the more generalized characters distinctive of the family to which the genus belongs. The same is true of the subdivisions of families into genera and of genera into species. Species were once the ultimate division, but it has been found advisable in recent years to subdivide some species into subspecies, since a species often exists as two or more recognizably different populations. This fact is best expressed by giving to each a separate name.

The scientific name of a bird consists of, first, the name of the genus to which it belongs, and, second, a specific name indicating a particular member of that genus. To designate a subspecies a third name is added. In this book the family name of the bird has been placed at the head of each descriptive section with the common name, and the name of the genus, species, and subspecies (if any) is given at the beginning of each description. Thus, for example, the Song Sparrow (Plate 88) is named *Melospiza melodia, Melospiza* being the name of the genus and *melodia* that of the species. The Song Sparrow found in the eastern United States is *Melospiza melodia melodia,* the second *melodia* indicating the subspecies or race found there.

In most cases subspecies are not sufficiently different to be identified in the field. For this reason field observers are being encouraged not to attempt identifications beyond the species. In fact, the latest checklist of North American birds gives common names only for the species. We are following this practice and only occasionally are subspecies mentioned in this book.

Mention is often made in the text of molting and of the various plumages that may be worn by the same bird during its life. Some birds are hatched naked, but others when hatched are covered with *natal down.* The natal down is sooner or later replaced by the *juvenal plumage,* which is acquired by a postnatal molt out of the downy stage. The juvenal plumage is lost by the postjuvenal molt and the plumage then attained is called the *postjuvenal,* the *fall,* or the *first fall and winter plumage.* During the latter part of the winter, or in the spring, many birds pass through a partial, and some through a complete, molt, called the *first prenuptial,* which is followed by the *first nuptial* or *first breeding plumage.* The brighter breeding plumage may be acquired toward spring by the wearing off of concealing feather margins, which is known as change by attrition or wear. After the nesting season is over there is a complete molt, the succeeding plumage being known as the *first postnuptial* or *second fall and winter plumage.* Most birds become fully adult at this time and have a complete molt each year after the breeding season. This is the usual sequence of molts and plumages, but there are many variations to be noted in different species. The annual, complete molt of adults following the breeding season is the only molt that can be predicted with certainty for any species until its full history is known.

One of the most important acquisitions of the bird student is a knowledge of bird songs and calls. In the identification of the smaller species it is of greater value than a knowledge of plumage markings. Each, of course, supplements the other, but more often than not it is the song and call notes that determine the presence and identity of a particular bird. Far more birds are heard than seen.

To learn the language of birds, however, is not an easy matter. Recent advances in the field recording of bird songs have resulted in excellent and very extensive recordings appearing on the market. These are invaluable aids to field recognition of bird songs. They are not, however, a substitute for watching the actual birds singing their songs, and each song and call must be traced patiently and carefully to its source, not once but many times, before it can be fully grasped by the memory. The beginner will be confused and discouraged by finding that not all individuals of the same species sing alike and that even the same bird may have a number of different songs. The solution is to learn primarily the quality of voice of each species, with only secondary attention to the sequence of the notes. The voice of an unseen friend is, under ordinary circumstances, readily recognized no matter what words are uttered. A person entirely devoid of musical sense can in this way, with close attention, learn to place accurately the songs and calls of many species without being able to reproduce or "carry in his head" any one of them. Occasionally, however, a bird will sing a song that is so entirely unlike its kind in every particular, even in quality of voice, that nothing but direct inspection will settle its identity.

The various call notes of the birds are their means of communication with one another or of expressing different emotions, such as fear, anxiety, or curiosity. The ability to interpret these sounds is inherited, and young birds just from the egg recognize the parents' notes of warning, or of assurance when danger is past.

Everyone who has learned to know birds at all is interested in their preservation. The total destruction of the Passenger Pigeon and the near extinction of other fine species are examples that should serve as warnings and call a halt to destruction before it is too late. More and more we are finding it difficult and ill-advised to distinguish between so-called "beneficial" and "injurious" species since there are no clear-cut distinctions. For this reason it seems best to protect all species and to control in numbers only those few where local conditions demand reduction.

The descriptions of birds given in this book include in practically all cases a note on the bird's food, so that its relative usefulness to man can be determined. Nearly all birds eat insects, and many are agents in the destruction of grasshoppers and caterpillars. Seed-eating birds perform a service also in destroying noxious weed seeds and the seeds of plants that tend to become too numerous. Even fish-eating birds are not to be condemned except under special conditions or when abnormally abundant.

In several states, hawks and owls are largely unprotected by law, and nearly every-one except the bird lover and the trained ornithologist considers it a commendable act to

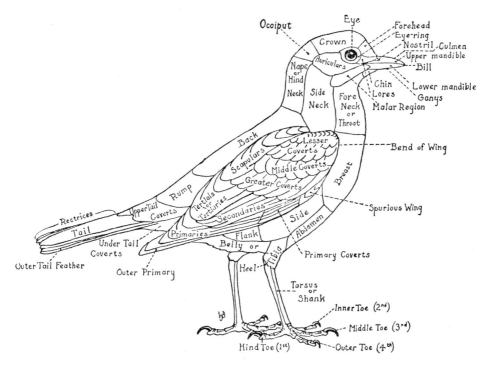

EXTERNAL TOPOGRAPHY OF A BIRD
This drawing gives the names of the different regions and parts as used in the descriptions.

kill them. As a matter of fact, only three or four species live chiefly on birds, while all species eat small mammals (mice, gophers, and rabbits), large insects, snakes, and other animals many of which are detrimental to man's interests. It is therefore not wise to kill hawks and owls indiscriminately.

In the text to follow the numbers in parentheses after the scientific names indicate in inches the length of the species, measuring from the tip of the bill to the end of the longest tail feather. The figures give the extremes, and when the sexes differ in size the range is from the shortest to the longest measurements, both sexes being considered together. This accounts for the great disparity in some instances.

By referring to the drawings of the external topography and tarsi of birds, repro-duced here from *The Birds of Minnesota,* the beginning student can gain a graphic definition of various technical terms used in the text.

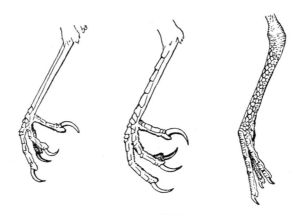

TARSI OF BIRDS
Left, a smooth or "booted" tarsus; middle, a scaled or scutellate tarsus; right, a reticulate tarsus.

A word may be added in regard to the relative parts taken by the artists in the painting of the originals of the plates here reproduced. With a single exception the paintings were all made for *The Birds of Minnesota.* The late Major Allan Brooks, well-known bird artist of Okanagan Landing, British Columbia, Canada, painted thirty-eight plates; Mr. Walter Alois Weber, formerly of the Chicago Natural History Museum, now with the *National Geographic Magazine,* Washington, D.C., painted twenty-seven; Mr. Walter John Breckenridge of the Museum of Natural History, University of Minnesota, painted fourteen; Mr. Francis Lee Jaques, formerly of the American Museum of Natural History, New York City, now of St. Paul, Minnesota, painted eight; Dr. George Miksch Sutton, formerly of Cornell University, Ithaca, New York, now at the University of Oklahoma, Norman, Oklahoma, painted four; and one plate, that of the Bobwhite, was painted many years ago by Mr. Louis Agassiz Fuertes and was presented to the author of this volume. The signatures on the plates will serve to inform those who are interested as to which paintings were made by each artist.

Thomas S. Roberts, 1934
with emendations by Walter J. Breckenridge, 1960

BIRD PORTRAITS IN COLOR

PLATE 1

LOONS (Family *Gaviidae*) AND GREBES (Family *Podicipedidae*)

Loons are large water birds of the Northern Hemisphere. They form a small group of four species, widely distributed, two of which are shown in the plate. Like most birds that live in the water they have dense, waterproof plumage, which is soft and velvety on the head and neck. They are expert divers and can swim rapidly for long distances under the surface, using both wings and legs to propel themselves. The legs are moved for the most part at right angles to the body, oar-fashion. Loons can rise from the water only by a long run on the surface, but when once awing are strong, swift, and direct fliers. Because their legs are short and of peculiar structure, placed far back on the body, loons are awkward creatures on land, either standing nearly erect or progressing by dropping onto the breast and propelling themselves by working the legs and wings vigorously. The tail is short and stiff, of eighteen to twenty feathers. The shanks or tarsi are much flattened laterally, which facilitates the movements of the legs through the water. The toes are large, the three front ones being fully webbed. The hind toe is small, is nearly on a level with the others, has a small flap, and is placed somewhat laterally. The loons' food consists almost entirely of fish, which they are able to catch in full pursuit, and for which they often descend to great depths.

Two large, dark, obscurely spotted eggs are laid in a rude nest on matted vegetation, on an old muskrat house, or on the shore near the water's edge. The silky, down-covered young are from the first expert swimmers and divers. At times they ride about on the backs of the parents, concealed among the long feathers at the base of the wings, and in this way may be transported from place to place. They develop slowly, and are not fully adult for two years or more. The sexes are alike in plumage. There are two complete molts each year, and the summer and winter plumages are different, the winter plumage being much duller. The wing feathers are all shed at the same time, when the birds are flightless for a short period.

The COMMON LOON or GREAT NORTHERN DIVER, *Gavia immer* (32-34.12), makes its summer home in the northern part of North America, in Greenland and Iceland, and in winter retreats beyond the lands of frozen water, reaching the Gulf of Mexico and Lower California in North America. In Europe it reaches the British Isles and occasionally farther south. The Common Loon is a beautiful and attractive object as it floats on the surface of some northern lake that is its summer home. With its echoing calls, weird laughter, droll courting antics, and wild races over the surface of the water, it preserves a note of the passing wilderness that should be reason for permitting it to live undisturbed.

The RED-THROATED LOON, *Gavia stellata* (24-27), is a still more northern bird, nearly cosmopolitan in its range, and comes southward into the United States in winter, chiefly coastwise. The fully adult bird in breeding plumage should be easily recognized, but in immature and winter plumage it may be confused with the Common Loon under similar conditions. The smaller size, more slender and slightly upturned bill, and white speckled back of the Red-throated may serve to distinguish it.

The WESTERN or SWAN-NECKED GREBE, *Aechmophorus occidentalis* (24-29), is shown with the loons for direct comparison, for it is possible to confuse it with immature loons. It is a more slender, longer-necked bird and prefers marshy lakes and sloughs to open water. It is a bird of the western half of North America, but it occurs casually throughout the Mississippi Valley and nests occasionally in the western part of the states bordering the Mississippi River on the west.

PLATE 1

WESTERN GREBE, BREEDING ADULT

COMMON LOON

IMMATURE   BREEDING ADULT

RED-THROATED LOON

FALL AND WINTER ADULTS

BREEDING ADULT

Scale about one-seventh

PLATE 2

GREBES (Family *Podicipedidae*)

Grebes are the water witches of the lakes, ponds, and streams. The smaller species are vulgarly known as hell-divers. In common with loons, grebes possess the curious power of sinking gradually into the water and maintaining themselves there at will, with only the head or bill above the surface. Certain of the common names have no doubt arisen from the mystery attaching to this seemingly complete disappearance, together with the fact that they can dive so quickly at the report of a firearm that it is almost impossible to hit them—they simply vanish instantly. They are water birds in the strictest sense of the term. They have small wings and no evident tail, and, although some species can and do fly long distances in migration, they are loath at other times to leave the water, resorting in the face of danger to diving. Like the loons they use the legs alternately in swimming, the strokes being delivered laterally at a considerable angle with the body, but they may use them together in bursts of speed or when maintaining an upright position in the water.

Grebes vary greatly in size. They are all smaller than loons, and one north Indian species is less than eight inches in length. The body is flatter than in ducks and the neck is long and slender. The plumage is hair-like, dense, closely appressed, and with a satiny sheen below. There is a narrow bare space from the eye to the base of the bill, largest in the Pied-billed. The shanks are compressed laterally as in the loons, but the front toes are flat and broad, with nails like human toenails; there are small webs at the base, and each toe is bordered with wide flaps. The sexes are alike, but the summer and winter plumages differ. The young are covered with fine down, varied in pattern, and are expert swimmers and divers right from the egg. They can "sink" and dive like the parents. They spend considerable time riding about on the backs of the old birds.

Grebes are noisy birds, uttering loud, resonant calls, and all have elaborate and curious mating antics. Several white or bluish-white eggs, which soon become much stained, are laid in a floating nest of decayed and water-soaked vegetation. When left by the parents the eggs are usually covered with a mat of wet debris. The food consists of fish, various water insects, crawfish, and other crustaceans. A curious habit of the grebes is the eating of their own feathers; more than half the contents of the stomach may consist of a ball of macerated feathers. These are even fed to the young.

There are nearly a score of species of grebes distributed throughout the globe. Six species are found in North America. The first three of the following four species occur in one or more races in both the Old and New Worlds. The fourth is confined to the New World.

The EARED GREBE, *Podiceps caspicus* (12.50-13.50), in North America occurs chiefly west of the Mississippi Valley, but enters the western parts of Kansas, Missouri, Iowa, and Minnesota, breeding not infrequently in the latter state.

The HORNED GREBE, *Podiceps auritus* (12.50-14.75), breeds in the northern part of North America, and winters chiefly in the southern United States.

The RED-NECKED or HOLBOELL'S GREBE, *Podiceps grisegena* (19.50-22.50), breeds in the northern part of North America, and retreats to the middle and southern United States in winter.

The PIED-BILLED GREBE or HELL-DIVER, *Podilymbus podiceps* (11.80-14.50), is the widely distributed North American race of a species that ranges throughout the Americas from northern Canada to Patagonia.

For the WESTERN GREBE see Plate 1.

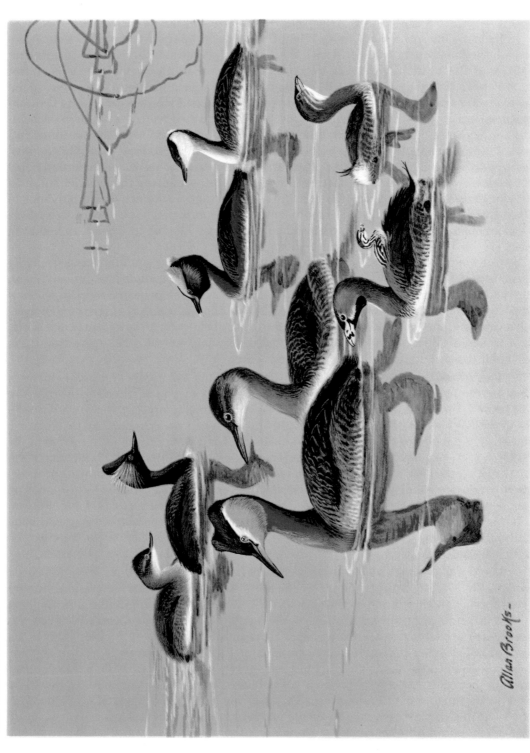

Allan Brooks-

EARED GREBE
IMMATURE   BREEDING ADULT

HORNED GREBE
BREEDING ADULT   FALL AND WINTER ADULT

RED-NECKED GREBE
BREEDING ADULT   IMMATURE

PIED-BILLED GREBE
IMMATURE

BREEDING ADULT AND CHICK

Scale about one-fifth

PLATE 3

PELICANS (Family *Pelecanidae*) AND CORMORANTS (Family *Phalacrocoracidae*)

Pelicans and cormorants, however much they may differ in general appearance, belong in the same order, *Pelecaniformes,* the Totipalmate Swimmers, the latter term signifying that all four toes are connected by a continuous web—a unique feature among birds.

Pelicans are large birds, four to six feet in length with a wingspread of eight to ten feet. There are six species, widely distributed in tropical and temperate regions. The conspicuous feature is an immense pouch below the large, hooked bill. This can be widened at the top to form a big scoop for catching fish. The wings are very large, the tail short and soft. They nest on the ground in colonies, and the young are cared for by the parents until full-grown. Pelicans are awkward on the ground but are stately and majestic birds as they move slowly over the surface of the water. In the air they are among the most accomplished and graceful of fliers as they soar in great circles high in the heavens or advance in flock-formation with slow steady movements of their immense wings. At rest the huge head is commonly drawn in with the pouch pressed closely against the breast. In flight the neck is folded vertically with the bill pointing forward.

Cormorants are almost world-wide in distribution. There are many species, most numerous in the tropics. With a few exceptions the color of the adult is iridescent black; the young are brown. There is no noticeable pouch as in the pelicans, but the gullet is capacious and dilatable. Cormorants are at home in the water and are expert and powerful swimmers, pursuing and catching their finny prey below the surface, using their short, stiff wings to aid in their swift progress. The tail is long, almost bare at the base, thus resembling somewhat the tail of a big woodpecker.

The WHITE PELICAN, *Pelecanus erythrorhynchos* (54-70), occurs at present chiefly in western temperate North America in summer, and in winter in northern California, the Gulf states, the coasts of Mexico, and Guatemala. The food is largely fish, which it scoops up in shallow water with its immense pouch, but it also eats many other aquatic creatures for which it dabbles on the bottom, swan-fashion. The food for the young is carried in the gullet, not in the pouch, and the nestlings secure it, with much struggling and commotion, by thrusting the head and neck far down into the open mouth of the parent. One to three, usually two, large dull white eggs are laid in a rude nest or depression in the ground. The young are hatched naked and blind but in time are covered with a pure white, fleecy down. The curious excrescence or "keel" on the bill, present in both sexes, is worn only during the mating and early nesting season. It, with the nuchal crest, is shed about the time the young are hatched, so the late summer, fall, and winter birds are not thus adorned.

The DOUBLE-CRESTED CORMORANT, "BLACK LOON," or "CROW-DUCK," *Phalacrocorax auritus* (30-35), breeds in southern Canada and the northern United States, and winters from Virginia to Florida and on the Gulf coast. It is now considerably reduced in numbers over much of its former breeding range in the northern United States, as the result of persecution on account of its fish-eating habits. It nests either on bare, rocky islands, or in the tops of tall trees in company with the Great Blue Heron. The narrow lateral crests that adorn both the male and female of this species are worn only during the mating season and are shed soon thereafter. Four to five dull bluish-white, chalk-roughened eggs are laid in a bulky, rough nest of coarse materials. The young are hatched naked and blind, but their bluish-black bodies are later covered with a dense black down. They are cared for by the parents until full-grown, and with much effort take the regurgitated fish from the mouth of the old bird.

DOUBLE-CRESTED CORMORANT
LATE NUPTIAL PLUMAGE   EARLY NUPTIAL PLUMAGE
AFTER SHEDDING CRESTS

WHITE PELICAN, BREEDING ADULT

Scale about one-eighth

PLATE 4

HERONS AND BITTERNS (Family *Ardeidae*)

The herons and bitterns belong to a large order (*Ciconiiformes*), which includes many notable birds such as the egrets, Maribou Storks of Africa and India, the Sacred Ibis of Egypt, and others equally interesting but of less fame. They are all long-legged, long-necked, aquatic birds with toes more or less webbed, the hind toe nearly on a level with the others, forming a foot suitable for perching. The herons and bitterns form a single family, which is divided into two subfamilies—the herons and egrets and the bitterns. Each group has representatives throughout the world. They are alike in having generally loose plumage, a straight, sharp-pointed bill, long and narrow heads sloping to the base of the bill, and the nail of the middle toe with a comb-like appendage on the inner border. The sexes are usually alike or nearly so in plumage; the female is smaller than the male; the young are generally different from the adults for the first year or two. Most species have plumes or other adornments, worn only during the breeding season. The young are cared for in the nest until grown and are fed by regurgitation. The herons usually nest in trees or bushes, the bitterns on or near the ground. The birds of this group have on the body small areas of curiously modified feathers called "powder-down patches." The feathers on these places are dull white, short, curly, and fragile in texture, and when rubbed between the fingers break off and form a fine powder, which has the feel of powdered talcum. There are three pairs in the herons, one pair on the breast, one on the flanks, and one on the lower belly, the latter pair lacking in the bitterns. They occur in other birds, notably in parrots. Their use is not fully understood.

The food of all the species consists in part of fish that they spear in shallow water with their dagger-like bills; frogs, tadpoles, crawfish, and various other water creatures; mice; and many insects, both land and aquatic.

The BLACK-CROWNED NIGHT HERON, *Nycticorax nycticorax* (23-28), as a species is world-wide in its distribution. One race occurs throughout the Americas from the northern United States and eastern Canada in the north to Argentina in the south. In winter it retreats from the colder parts of its range to milder climes.

The Night Heron, usually a common bird where it dwells, is rather nocturnal in habits. It nests in large colonies, commonly in low trees, but on the prairies it adapts itself to the very different conditions found in quill-reed and rush swamps. The eggs are pale blue, unmarked, three to six in number. It has been called the "Qua-bird" or "Squawk" because of the explosive notes it utters as it flies about the marshes in the evening.

The GREEN HERON, *Butorides virescens* (17-19), is a bird of the New World. In its several races it is found over most of the United States, southeastern Canada, Mexico, Central America, and the outlying islands. The race occurring in the upper Mississippi Valley breeds east of the Rocky Mountains from southern Canada on the north to Central America on the south, retreating in winter to the southern part of its range. It is for the most part a solitary bird, nesting in bushes or trees near water, and laying three to six pale blue, unmarked eggs. It is commonly found along the shores of woodland lakes, ponds, and streams, is alert and shy, and when disturbed hurries off with an emphatic *qua-qua* or *peu-ah, peu-ah*. In strong light the back appears blue rather than green. In the mating season the male has bright coral-red legs and feet, which are conspicuous as they trail out behind in flight.

For the GREAT BLUE HERON see Plate 26.

BLACK-CROWNED NIGHT HERON
ADULT FEMALE   ADULT MALE   IMMATURE

GREEN HERON
IMMATURE   ADULT FEMALE   ADULT MALE

Scale about one-fifth

PLATE 5

BITTERNS (Family *Ardeidae*)

Bitterns differ from the true herons in having ten soft tail feathers instead of twelve stiffish ones; only two instead of three pairs of powder-down tracts; the outer toe shorter instead of longer than the inner one; the front toenails long and slender and little curved instead of short and much curved; and no head plumes or white plumage in any species. They are solitary birds and nest on or near the ground.

The AMERICAN BITTERN, *Botaurus lentiginosus* (25-28), is an inhabitant of North and Central America, breeding over most of Canada and the United States and wintering in the southern United States, north on the Pacific coast to British Columbia, and in Mexico, Panama, and the outlying islands. It may wander accidentally to Greenland, Iceland, Great Britain, and the Azores. The American Bittern is a bird of the marshes and sloughs, solitary in habit, building a nest of grasses on the ground, and laying three to five, rarely more, greenish-buff, unmarked eggs. The young are fed at first a partly digested, nearly liquid pap, but later the growing youngsters seize the parent's bill crosswise and with much effort the regurgitated mass of insects, frogs, and other animal food is transferred to the infant's throat.

The male is famous for its remarkable and unmusical love song, for, strange as it may seem, this is undoubtedly its real nature. In the late spring and early summer there comes from the meadow or bog a series of resonant, pumping notes sounding not unlike the noise made by the working of a loose wooden suction pump or, when heard at a distance, like the strokes of a wooden mallet driving a stake in squashy soil. From this comes the common names "Thunder-pump," "Bog-pumper," and "Stake-driver." This "song" has been variously represented in words by different authors, the most common being *pump-er-lunk* when heard entire near at hand, the strongly accented last syllable giving, at a distance, the stake-driving sound. Mr. Bradford Torrey and others have happily rendered it *plum-pudd'n,* the *plum* sound prolonged and a strong accent on the *pudd'n,* the lips being kept nearly closed throughout. The contortions of the bird during the delivery of this vocal performance are an interesting and strange spectacle, worth a special effort to see. The sound is made, as usual with birds, in the voice box at the lower end of the windpipe but is greatly increased in volume by passing over a drum-like arrangement produced by the inflation with air of the upper part of the gullet. During the courting season the male may be seen strutting or pursuing the female with two large fluffy tufts of white feathers showing on the back between the bases of the wings. At other times these are concealed on the sides beneath the wings.

The LEAST BITTERN, *Ixobrychus exilis* (11-14.25), is confined to the Americas, ranging from southern Canada to Colombia, Brazil, and Paraguay in South America. The eastern United States race breeds from southern Ontario south to the West Indies and southern Mexico and west to Saskatchewan and North Dakota. It winters in the southeastern United States, the West Indies, and through Central America to Brazil.

The Least Bittern is an elusive and eerie denizen of dense reed and rush swamps. Except on rare occasions it spends its life hidden away in such almost inaccessible places that it is rarely seen by the casual observer. Its notes are subdued, mostly cooing in quality, of little carrying power and easily lost in the general chorus of the average marshland. The nest is a frail, loosely canopied affair, supported among the stems of the reeds. The eggs are three to six in number, pale greenish-white or bluish-white.

AMERICAN BITTERN, ADULT
LEAST BITTERN
FEMALE   MALE
Scale about one-third

PLATE 6

SWANS, GEESE, AND DUCKS (Family *Anatidae*)

However much these birds may differ in external appearance they are alike in certain structural characters and are placed in a single family of the order *Anseriformes*. They are, with a few exceptions, typically aquatic in habits. They agree in having the edges of both mandibles furnished with tooth-like projections that interlock when the bill is closed, forming a strainer and allowing the water to escape from the mouth when the birds are feeding. The legs in most species are placed near the middle of the body so that the walking gait is a waddle. During the molting period all the main flight feathers and the tail feathers are shed simultaneously, rendering the bird flightless for a short time. Swans differ from the other members of the group in having the neck longer than the body and the face partly bare of feathers. All are big white birds except the Black Swan of Australia and the Black-necked Swan of southern South America. Geese have the neck shorter than the body and the face is entirely feathered.

The WHISTLING SWAN, *Olor columbianus* (48-55), is a North American species, breeding chiefly north of the Arctic Circle and migrating in winter to the southern coastal regions of the United States. It still passes through the interior in flocks of considerable size. It was the Trumpeter Swan, now nearly extinct, that once bred in the northern United States and southern Canada. In the two American species of swans the windpipe is extensively coiled in the keel of the breastbone, which imparts volume to their loud, far-carrying calls. The yellow spot in the bare space in front of the eye in the adult Whistler is usually regarded as a distinguishing mark between it and the Trumpeter but it is not entirely reliable. The birds that have it are all Whistlers, but not all birds without it are Trumpeters.

The CANADA GOOSE or HONKER, *Branta canadensis* (34-43), breeds over much of Canada from the arctic to the northern United States, but is now greatly reduced in numbers in the latter area. It was once a common summer resident throughout the north central United States, but is at present almost entirely a migrant there. There are many forms of the Canada Goose varying from birds of about Mallard-size with stubby bills to birds weighing fourteen to sixteen pounds. These represent breeding populations from different areas, mainly in arctic Canada, and are practically impossible to distinguish in the field. As a species they are found in winter as far south as central Mexico.

The SNOW GOOSE, *Chen hyperborea* (26.29-30.55), breeds in the American arctic region and winters in the southern United States to central Mexico. The Greater Snow Goose is an Atlantic coast bird and does not occur in the interior.

The BLUE GOOSE, *Chen caerulescens* (25-30), breeds on Baffin Island and Southampton Island and migrates chiefly through the Mississippi Valley to its main wintering ground on the coast of Louisiana. It often mingles with the Snow Goose in migration. Both the Snow and Blue Geese differ from the others in the plate in having the edges of the mandibles on each side separated or rolled back so as to show the serrations—"grinning." The Blue Goose is considered by many ornithologists to be a dark color phase of the Snow Goose.

The WHITE-FRONTED GOOSE, *Anser albifrons* (26.70-30), is nearly cosmopolitan in its range. It breeds in western arctic Canada, on the west coast of Greenland, in Iceland, Lapland, and on the arctic coast of Siberia; in North America, it winters in the western United States, the Gulf coast, and Mexico, and in the Eastern Hemisphere as far south as India and northern Africa. Because of its peculiar cry the White-fronted Goose has been called the Laughing Goose, and by hunters is variously known as the Speckled Brant, Gray Brant, Gray Wavey, and Speckle-belly.

PLATE 6

WHISTLING SWAN
ADULT   IMMATURE

WHITE-FRONTED GOOSE
ADULT

CANADA GOOSE
ADULT

SNOW GOOSE
IMMATURE   ADULT

BLUE GOOSE
ADULT

Scale of foreground figures about one-eighth

PLATE 7

SURFACE-FEEDING DUCKS (Family *Anatidae*)

The ducks belonging to this group, shown on this and the two following plates, are called surface-feeding ducks because, though they can dive readily on occasion, they have the habit of feeding from the surface, tipping up the body and dabbling for food on the bottom in shallow water or scooping it up from the surface with their broad, strainer-like bills. This habit has earned for them the names "Dabbling-ducks" and "Puddle-ducks." The fine, comb-like fringes on the edges of the mandibles are especially well developed in these ducks. Many of the most brilliantly colored species belong here and a characteristic feature is the bright, usually iridescent, patch of feathers in the middle of the wing, called the "speculum." The adult males in the summer molt their showy feathers and pass through a concealing or "eclipse" plumage, in which they resemble the dull-colored females. This plumage carries them in comparative safety over the flightless period, following which the full nuptial dress is again assumed. The diet consists of almost anything edible but much more than half of the food is vegetable matter, the remainder including mollusks, crustaceans, fish, and many insects. There are about seventy species belonging to this group, widely distributed throughout the world. Thirteen species occur regularly in North America.

The MALLARD, *Anas platyrhynchos* (21-24.50), is found in the breeding season throughout most of the Northern Hemisphere, retreating in winter in the Old World as far as northern Africa, India, southern China, and Japan, and in the New World reaching Florida and Mexico. The Mallard builds a nest of coarse grasses and rushes either in a marsh or on the adjoining upland, and lays eight to twelve greenish or grayish-buff eggs, which during the absence of the parent are covered with down plucked from the breast of the female. More or less down enters into the construction of the nests of all the *Anatidae* and serves to protect the eggs from cold and exposure.

The BLACK DUCK, *Anas rubripes* (21.75-24.50), known among sportsmen in the Midwest as the Black or Dusky Mallard, breeds chiefly in eastern Canada and the northeastern United States, wintering on the Atlantic coast from New England southward and in the interior from the Great Lakes to the Gulf coast. In the eastern part of its breeding range it replaces to a considerable extent the Mallard. There are yellow-billed, red-legged birds and dark-billed, dark-legged birds, which are now known to represent age differences.

The PINTAIL, *Anas acuta* (21.75-30), is found in both the Old and New Worlds. It breeds throughout most of arctic and temperate North America, wintering as far south as northern South America and the West Indies. The Pintail has the widest breeding range of any North American duck. It usually nests on dry uplands.

The AMERICAN WIDGEON or BALDPATE, *Mareca americana* (18.75-21), is confined to North and Central America, breeding chiefly in Canada west of Hudson Bay and more sparingly in the northern United States from the Great Lakes westward; it winters over most of the United States to the West Indies, Panama, and Costa Rica. It nests on dry ground near water.

The GADWALL or GRAY DUCK *Anas strepera* (19.60-21.50), is nearly worldwide in its range, breeding throughout northern Eurasia, western Canada, and the northern United States west of Hudson Bay and the Great Lakes; it migrates in winter to northern Africa and southern China in the Old World, and to the southern United States and Mexico in the New World, north on the Pacific coast to British Columbia. The Gadwall nests on dry ground near a lake or slough.

PLATE 7

BIRD PORTRAITS IN COLOR

Allan Brooks-

AMERICAN WIDGEON, ADULTS (FLYING)
MALE   FEMALE

MALLARD, ADULTS
MALE   FEMALE

GADWALL, ADULTS
FEMALE   MALE (FLYING)

BLACK DUCK, ADULT

AMERICAN PINTAIL, ADULTS
MALE   FEMALE

Scale about one-seventh

PLATE 8

SURFACE-FEEDING DUCKS (Family *Anatidae*)

The GREEN-WINGED TEAL, *Anas carolinensis* (12.75-15.75), is found throughout most of North America, breeding commonly in Canada west of Hudson Bay and more sparingly in the northern United States; it winters in the southern United States, Mexico, the West Indies, and northern Central America. A closely related species, the Common Teal, occurs throughout most of the Old World.

The Green-winged Teal is the smallest of our ducks. It arrives earlier in the spring and leaves later in the fall than the Blue-wing. It is now an uncommon breeding bird in the upper Mississippi Valley but still appears spring and fall in swiftly flying flocks, darting and whirling about in erratic fashion. The tiny Green-wing is courageous and audacious enough to wait upon the larger diving ducks and steal a portion of the wild celery that they bring to the surface. The females of both the Green-winged and Blue-winged Teal quack something like the female Mallard only less loudly, while the drakes, as is usual among ducks, utter much less pretentious and feebler notes. The nest is on the ground in meadows or the adjacent upland.

The BLUE-WINGED TEAL, *Anas discors* (15-16.35), breeds nearly throughout North America and winters in the southern United States, Mexico, the Bahamas, West Indies, the coasts of northern South America, and in Brazil and central Chile. This teal is one of the few American ducks that pass beyond the equator in the southward migration.

Though much reduced in numbers the Blue-wing is still the commonest summer resident duck in the upper Mississippi Valley. The nest is in a thick tussock in a wet marsh or meadow or on the upland near by. The white face-bar of the spring male is lacking in the fall, as the full nuptial plumage is not acquired until the winter or early spring. The teal is credited by hunters with being the swiftest flier among our ducks. Certainly a single bird, going with the wind, seems to be going almost too fast to be followed with the eye, and only an expert can stop such a bird with a shot except by chance. Airplane tests have shown that fifty to sixty miles an hour is the usual speed of migrating ducks.

The CINNAMON TEAL, *Anas cyanoptera* (15.50-17), is exceptional in having two breeding areas, separated by some 2000 miles—one in western North America and one in southern South America; it winters south and north of the breeding ranges; it is casual in the eastern United States, including the Mississippi Valley.

The SHOVELER or SPOONBILL, *Spatula clypeata* (18.50-20.75), is one of the most widely distributed of ducks, occurring in both the Old and the New Worlds. In North America it breeds in the United States and Canada, chiefly west of the Great Lakes; it winters in the southern United States and West Indies to northern South America and Hawaii, north on the Pacific coast to British Columbia. In the Old World it breeds over most of northern Eurasia, and in winter occurs as far south as northern Africa on the west and Japan and China on the east.

The big spoon-shaped bill of the Shoveler marks it well among other ducks. It feeds in shallow water, tipping up and scraping the mud from the bottom, straining out the food particles by means of the wonderfully developed interlocking laminae or "teeth" that fringe the edges of both mandibles. The food is more largely animal than is the case with most shoal-water ducks, about 34 per cent being of this nature. The nest is on the ground in meadows or marshes or on the adjacent uplands.

PLATE 8

BIRD PORTRAITS IN COLOR

GREEN-WINGED TEAL
IMMATURE

CINNAMON TEAL
MALE

GREEN-WINGED TEAL
FEMALE

BLUE-WINGED TEAL
FEMALE

BLUE-WINGED TEAL
MALE

SHOVELER
MALE

FEMALE

Scale of foreground figures about one-seventh

GREEN-WINGED TEAL
FEMALE

MALE

SURFACE-FEEDING DUCKS (Family *Anatidae*)

The WOOD DUCK, *Aix sponsa* (17.75-20), is a bird of temperate North America, breeding throughout most of the United States and southern Canada and wintering mainly in the southern United States to Jamaica and central Mexico.

The male Wood Duck is unquestionably the most beautiful member of its family in America, and in the brilliancy, variety, and exquisite pattern of its colors is rivaled by few, if any, of its kind in the world. The drake in full display, floating proudly on some quiet woodland pool, is a most gorgeous and dazzlingly handsome sight. His mate, by contrast, is quiet and plain in dress, and during the summer eclipse the drake also assumes for a time simple colors resembling the female. The short, vertical, white line dividing the gray on the side of the head is retained and, aside from the more brilliant bill and wing-coverts, is the chief remaining character by which the sex may be determined.

The Wood, Carolina, or Summer Duck, as it has been variously called, was once an abundant summer resident in all the upper Mississippi Valley but of late years has been greatly reduced in numbers. However, under rigid protection by both federal and state laws it is coming back fairly well.

The favorite haunts of the Wood Duck are woodland lakes, quiet willow-bordered streams, flooded bottomlands studded with dead and decaying trees, and wood-fringed sloughs and marshes. It is seldom found at any season on large bodies of water. It seems out of place in open country but is not infrequent about the sparsely wooded shores of prairie lakes.

When startled the Wood Duck rises abruptly from the water with a quick upward spring, gaining speed very rapidly. Once on the wing its flight is swift and silent. When disturbed it utters a complaining, somewhat squeaky protest, *ho-eek', ho-eek', ho-eek',* and when at dusk a flock comes circling in over a chosen resting place this same note may be heard as the ducks call down to others of their kind already there. During the daytime the Wood Duck spends much of its time resting on the trunks of fallen trees and other debris about shaded pools and along the banks of streams.

The nesting place is a hole in a tree or stub or, it may be, in a box placed for its use. The site is usually near or over water, and the entrance is six to thirty feet above the ground. Strange to say, the duck can enter a hole less than four inches in diameter. There is no nest except such refuse as may be in the cavity with the addition of much down from the duck's breast. There has been much difference of opinion as to how this and other tree-nesting ducks get the young safely out of the nest. The truth seems to be that in most instances the young get themselves down. Climbing to the opening with the aid of their sharp little toenails they launch themselves into the air and flutter down like little puffballs, landing unharmed in the water or on the ground as the case may be. When one makes up its mind to go, the others follow quickly, and in two or three minutes all are out and swim or waddle off with the parents to be cared for until full-grown. Although the female hatches the eggs alone, careful observation has shown that the male sometimes remains in the vicinity and after the young are out makes one of the family party.

Over 90 per cent of the food of the Wood Duck consists of vegetable substances. Nuts enter largely into the diet, to secure which the birds visit wooded uplands. Acorns are a favorite item and open oak forests are popular feeding places. Here the birds run hither and thither beneath the trees picking up the fallen nuts, and when startled at such times they spring from the ground in a compact flock and thread their way with surprising ease in and out among the crowded trees.

WOOD DUCK

ADULT MALE

ADULT FEMALE   MALE IN ECLIPSE

Scale about one-fifth

PLATE 9

DIVING DUCKS (Family *Anatidae*)

The ducks belonging to this group, unlike the surface-feeding species, get their food by diving for it in open water; therefore they are commonly seen on bodies of clear water rather than in sloughs or marshy places. The surface-feeding ducks can rise or spring directly from the water and are soon under way, but the diving ducks must first take a longer or shorter run on the surface before getting into the air. This fact makes it really necessary for them to live in open water. To facilitate diving the feet are larger and the legs shorter and placed farther back on the body than in the surface-feeders. The hind toe is well developed and provided with a wide, membranous flap or lobe instead of being slender and bare as in the latter group. There is considerable diversity in external appearance and minor details in the widely distributed species and subspecies which occur in North America. The wing-patch or speculum, if present, is usually white or gray, and the eclipse plumage in the plainer species is less evident. The sexes differ in plumage. All the ducks grouped on this plate build nests of coarse materials among dense rushes and reeds where the water is a foot or more in depth.

The REDHEAD, *Aythya americana* (19.25-23), is a North American duck and breeds mainly in the north central United States and in Canada from southern Manitoba westward; it winters chiefly in the southern United States along the Atlantic and Gulf coasts and north on the Pacific coast to British Columbia. The Redhead still nests in fair numbers in the northern prairie states and adjacent provinces.

The CANVAS-BACK, *Aythya valisineria* (20-24), is, like the Redhead, a North American duck and breeds chiefly in the prairie regions of the north central United States and the prairie provinces of Canada; it winters mainly in the southern United States along the Atlantic and Gulf coasts, in central Mexico, and north on the Pacific coast to British Columbia. The Canvas-back was once a common nesting bird in the more open portions of the upper Mississippi Valley states but is now largely a migrant there.

The RING-NECKED DUCK, *Aythya collaris* (15.50-18), is North American in its range and breeds mainly in the north central United States and south central Canada west of the Great Lakes and Ontario; it winters in the southern United States, the Bahamas, south through Mexico to Guatemala, north on the Pacific coast to southern British Columbia. It was formerly a common breeding duck in the upper Mississippi Valley and the neighboring states but has been greatly reduced in numbers as a summer resident in recent years.

The LESSER SCAUP or LITTLE BLUE-BILL, *Aythya affinis* (15-18), breeds mainly in southern Alaska and western Canada east to Hudson Bay, less commonly in the north central United States and southeastern Ontario; it winters in the southern United States and south along the coasts of Mexico and Central America to Panama, north on the Pacific coast to British Columbia. The Lesser Scaup is still a numerous migrant in the upper Mississippi Valley but is now much less frequent as a summer resident.

The GREATER SCAUP or LARGE BLUE-BILL, *Aythya marila* (17-20.75), is found in both the Old and New Worlds, the New World bird being regarded as a separate subspecies. It is a more northern-breeding duck than the Lesser Scaup and in winter is found chiefly along the seacoasts of the Northern Hemisphere. It is much less common than the Lesser Scaup from which it is very difficult to distinguish.

All the ducks shown on this plate are very highly regarded as game birds, the Canvas-back and Redhead being especially favored. The flesh is darker and less delicately flavored than in the surface-feeding ducks but has a special appeal for many palates.

PLATE 9

BIRD PORTRAITS IN COLOR

RING-NECKED DUCK, ADULTS

FEMALE   MALE

GREATER SCAUP, ADULT MALE (FLYING)

CANVAS-BACK, ADULTS   LESSER SCAUP, ADULTS

FEMALE   MALE   FEMALE   MALE

REDHEAD, ADULTS

FEMALE   MALE

Scale about one-seventh

PLATE 10

DIVING DUCKS (Family *Anatidae*)

The ducks on this and the succeeding two plates are preeminently open-water diving birds. They are rarely found anywhere except on the larger, clear-water lakes and rivers. Several of them are well represented in winter in the northern United States wherever there is open water, as on the Great Lakes.

The COMMON or AMERICAN GOLDEN-EYE or WHISTLER, *Bucephala clangula americana* (16.75-20), breeds in the extreme northern United States and in Canada to tree-limit entirely across the continent; it winters in the interior from the northern limit of open water, especially the Great Lakes, to the southern United States on both seacoasts, and rarely to the Gulf and northern Mexico. It is represented in the Old World by a very similar race, which breeds in the far north and winters in southern Europe and Asia.

The Golden-eye nests in a hollow tree or stub, often at a considerable distance from the ground. There is no nest except such refuse as may be in the cavity and an abundance of white down and feathers from the body of the bird. In flight the wings make a loud whistling noise, from which comes the common name Whistler or Whistle-wing. The food consists of over 90 per cent animal matter. The Golden-eye is a large, heavy duck but as a game bird it does not rank high, for the flesh is not very palatable.

BARROW'S GOLDEN-EYE, *Bucephala islandica* (20-23), breeds in the mountains of northwestern North America, in Labrador, Greenland, and Iceland, and winters on the North Atlantic and Pacific coasts, in the interior south sparingly and irregularly to the United States. It is a rare duck in the upper Mississippi Valley.

Barrow's Golden-eye is similar in habits to the American Golden-eye and is not easily distinguished from that species at a distance. The crescent-shaped white spot on the face of the male Barrow's is the best field mark when it can be made out. The females are indistinguishable.

The BUFFLE-HEAD or BUTTER-BALL, *Bucephala albeola* (12.25-15), is a North American duck. It breeds now chiefly north of the United States from Alaska to Hudson Bay; it winters along the Pacific coast and across the continent south of the northern limit of open water, to the South Atlantic and Gulf coasts; it is casual in Bermuda, the West Indies, and Hawaii. It is an early spring and late fall migrant in the upper Mississippi Valley.

Next to the Green-winged Teal the Buffle-head is the smallest of our ducks. It loves the rough open water and is an expert diver, swimming rapidly under water in pursuit of the fish that form a considerable part of its diet. It rises from the water more easily than most of the diving ducks, flies rapidly, and alights with a splash, skidding along some distance before coming to rest. It is often very fat but the flesh is not especially palatable, and this, with its small size, makes it an indifferent game bird. It nests in a hole in a tree like the Golden-eyes.

The OLD-SQUAW or LONG-TAILED DUCK, *Clangula hyemalis* (21-23), is a winter visitant in the interior of the United States, chiefly the Great Lakes, where it is common from late fall until late spring. It is circumpolar in its distribution, breeding in the far north and wintering in North America on the Atlantic and Pacific coasts, and in the Old World in southern Europe and Asia.

The Old-squaw is a duck of the arctic regions and northern seacoasts, coming south in winter and living under conditions similar to its boreal home. It is a swift flier and an expert diver, having been taken in nets at a depth of over a hundred feet. Its food is almost entirely animal matter and its flesh is dark, rank, and unpalatable.

PLATE 10

BIRD PORTRAITS IN COLOR

OLD SQUAW (FLYING)
MALE, BREEDING ADULT
MALE, WINTER ADULT
FEMALE, BREEDING ADULT

BARROW'S GOLDEN-EYE
MALE

BUFFLE-HEAD
MALE
FEMALE

COMMON GOLDEN-EYE
MALE

FEMALE

Scale of foreground figures about one-seventh

PLATE 11

SCOTERS AND RUDDY DUCK (Family *Anatidae*)

Scoters are large, uniformly dark-colored ducks, varied by a white wing-patch in one species. The males in breeding plumage have varicolored bills, swollen at the base in two species. The feather outline at the base of the bill distinguishes the species in any plumage. They are expert divers, feeding almost entirely on small fish, mussels, crawfish, and other aquatic creatures. On the North Atlantic coast scoters are called "coots" and coot-shooting is a favorite sport, but the flesh is not very palatable even when specially prepared.

The three species of scoters are represented in the upper Mississippi Valley and the neighboring states. The White-winged Scoter is there a fairly regular spring and fall migrant but is not numerous except occasionally on Lake Superior, where it may appear in the spring in flocks of considerable size. Most of these leave in May but a few may remain through the summer, though there is no evidence that the bird nests there. In the fall it reappears in large numbers and remains until cold weather. The other two species are rare stragglers inland, but on Lake Superior may be present in flocks numbering several dozen birds and are at times intermingled in the same flock.

The SURF SCOTER, *Melanitta perspicillata* (18-22), breeds mainly in northwestern Alaska and northern Canada from coast to coast; it winters chiefly on the North American seacoasts, on the Great Lakes, and sparingly farther south. It is casual in Europe.

The WHITE-WINGED SCOTER, *Melanitta deglandi* (19.50-22.50), breeds in Alaska and in Canada from coast to coast, south to British Columbia and southern Manitoba, and in the United States in northeastern Washington and central North Dakota. It winters on both coasts and irregularly and less commonly southward in the interior. The west coast birds have been separated as a subspecies and there are two widely distributed similar races in Europe and Asia.

The COMMON or BLACK SCOTER, *Oidemia nigra* (17-21), breeds in Alaska and northern Canada from coast to coast and winters on the Atlantic and Pacific coasts regularly as far south as New Jersey and southern California, in the interior to the Great Lakes and casually farther south, and also from the Commander Islands to Japan and China.

The little RUDDY DUCK, *Oxyura jamaicensis* (15-17), belongs to a small group (subfamily *Oxyurinae*) of some half-dozen species widely scattered throughout the world and known as the Masked Ducks—sometimes called Spiny-tails, because the tail feathers are narrow, stiff, and sharp-pointed. The North American Ruddy breeds mainly in the prairie sloughs and rush-grown lakes of central and western Canada and the north central United States but occurs more or less irregularly throughout most of North America south through Lower California to Guatemala; it winters on the Atlantic coast south of Maryland, in the Bahamas, and on the Pacific coast to Mexico and Costa Rica.

In most ways the little Ruddy is a unique member of the North American duck tribe. In its dense plumage with a silvery sheen below, its preference for diving and swimming under water rather than taking wing, and its helplessness on land, it resembles the grebes. Its stiff, bare, spiny tail is almost like the tail of a woodpecker, and when the bird is sitting on the water this is usually carried tilted forward at a considerable angle with the back, producing the appearance of a little toy duck. The male remains with the female during incubation; the eclipse plumage is worn until spring; the female is silent, the male vocal during the mating period; and the male has an air sac in the neck connected with the windpipe, which can be inflated during the mating display. All this is very different from other North American ducks.

PLATE 11

SURF SCOTER
MALE, BREEDING ADULT

WHITE-WINGED SCOTER
MALE, BREEDING ADULT
FEMALE, BREEDING ADULT

AMERICAN SCOTER
MALE, BREEDING ADULT

RUDDY DUCK
MALE, BREEDING ADULT
FEMALE, BREEDING ADULT

Scale of foreground figures about one-ninth

PLATE 12

MERGANSERS OR FISH DUCKS (Family *Anatidae*)

The members of this group may be recognized at once by their narrow bills with toothlike serrations on the edges and the upper mandible hooked. There is another group of narrow-billed ducks called Torrent Ducks but they are found in the Andes Mountains in South America. Adult mergansers have crested heads and the sexes are unlike. There are seven species, widely distributed throughout the world. Three occur in North America. The mergansers are chiefly open-water ducks and expert divers, living largely on fish that they catch by pursuing them below the surface like loons, grebes, and cormorants. Their flesh is hardly edible and they are of little economic value but not necessarily harmful. Most fish-eating birds consume chiefly small fish that devour the eggs and fry of more valuable species, so that limiting their numbers is really a benefit to man. Male mergansers have a well-developed eclipse, which appears late, and the return to full plumage is slow. Young males may be two or three years in reaching fully adult plumage, as in the case of the Hooded Merganser.

The HOODED MERGANSER, LITTLE FISH DUCK, or LITTLE SAW-BILL, *Lophodytes cucullatus* (17-19), is a North American duck, breeding locally from coast to coast throughout most of the United States and southern Canada; it winters mainly in the southern United States, Cuba, and central eastern Mexico, less commonly farther north; it is accidental in Bermuda, Wales, and Ireland. The great fan-shaped crest of the male Hooded Merganser, with its jet-black border and brilliant white center, is an adornment equaled by no other member of the North American duck tribe. It is not until full maturity, after two or three years, that this adornment attains its full development. Normally the Hooded Merganser nests in a cavity in a tree, like the Wood Duck, and in the breeding season it seeks wooded ponds and lakes or flooded bottomlands where suitable sites can be found.

The RED-BREASTED MERGANSER, RED-BREASTED GOOSANDER, RED-BREASTED SHELDRAKE, *Mergus serrator* (19.75-24), in North America breeds in Alaska, in Canada, and less commonly in the northern tier of the United States from coast to coast and in Greenland; it winters mainly along the Atlantic, Pacific, and Gulf coasts and from the Great Lakes southward. In the Eastern Hemisphere it occurs widely over Europe, Asia, and northern Africa; it is casual in Bermuda, Cuba, and Hawaii. The Red-breasted Merganser nests on the ground, usually near the water's edge, concealing its nest beneath grass or low-hanging branches of evergreens or under boulders or driftwood.

The COMMON or AMERICAN MERGANSER, BIG FISH DUCK, BIG SHELDRAKE, BIG SAW-BILL, or GOOSANDER, *Mergus merganser* (22-26.50), breeds in Canada and the northern United States entirely across the continent, and southward to the Mexican border in the Rocky Mountains; it winters over most of the United States and southern Canada where there is open water, to the Gulf and northern Mexico; it is represented in the Old World by two subspecies which are widely distributed over Europe and Asia. The Common Merganser or Goosander is one of the largest, and the drake one of the handsomest, of our ducks. It remains through the winter in the northern United States where there is sufficient open water. The nest is on the ground near water, concealed among overhanging bushes, boulders, or debris; or it may be in a cavity in a tree or cliff, or even in a deserted building or a crow's nest. This is the large merganser seen commonly in the nesting season in the Lake Superior region, the Red-breasted being rarely found there at that time of the year.

HOODED MERGANSER, ADULTS
FEMALE   MALE
RED-BREASTED MERGANSER, ADULTS
MALE
FEMALE

COMMON MERGANSER, ADULTS
FEMALE   MALE

Scale about one-seventh

PLATE 13

VULTURES (Family *Cathartidae*) AND HAWKS (Family *Accipitridae*)

The birds shown on this and the succeeding six plates belong to an order known as the diurnal birds of prey (*Falconiformes*) to distinguish them from the nocturnal birds of prey, the owls (*Strigiformes*). The two groups were formerly associated under the name *Raptores* but for structural reasons are now widely separated. The diurnal birds of prey constitute a very large group, there being no fewer than 287 species and 413 subspecies listed in Peters' *Birds of the World*. They are found in all parts of the world and differ greatly in size and appearance. They are alike generally in being of robust build with short, strong, hooked, lobed, or toothed bills, provided with sharp cutting edges. At the base of the upper mandible is a soft, wax-like structure called a cere, in which the nostrils open (except in the Osprey). The eyes are placed laterally and are protected by a bony ridge or shield immediately above them. The legs are generally short and the feet are provided with sharp, curved talons (except in the vultures). The sexes are usually alike but the female is commonly much larger than the male. In most species the young differ greatly from the adults and it may require two or three years for them to acquire mature plumage.

These birds are strictly carnivorous and most species are valuable aids to the agriculturist in keeping in check injurious rodents and insects. Nearly all will take birds on occasion but there are only three or four species that live to any considerable extent on such food. It is a serious mistake to destroy all species of hawks indiscriminately as has been done for so many years.

The RED-SHOULDERED HAWK, *Buteo lineatus* (17.50-22), is a North American species, breeding in southern Canada, throughout the United States, and in northwestern Mexico. The northern birds retire southward in winter. The resident birds of the west coast and southern United States have been separated as subspecies.

The MARSH HAWK, *Circus cyaneus hudsonius* (19.50-24), has a wide range throughout North America, breeding in Alaska, Canada, and most of the United States, and wintering south as far as the West Indies, Central America, and rarely northern South America. It is represented in Eurasia by very similar forms, which are now regarded as subspecies of this species. The Marsh Hawk has survived the general slaughter of hawks in greater numbers than almost any other species. The nest is placed on the ground, usually in a marsh. The white patch at the base of the tail is a good field mark.

The SWALLOW-TAILED KITE, *Elanoides forficatus* (19.50-25), formerly bred locally from northwestern Minnesota southeastward to South Carolina and south through eastern Mexico to Central America; it winters south of the United States. It was once a common summer resident locally in the northern United States, but has now disappeared almost entirely from the northern part of its former range. It is represented in Central and South America by a closely allied race. It is regrettable that this handsome and interesting bird has disappeared from our northern forests where once it dwelt in numbers. A considerable part of its food consists of snakes, which it carries aloft and eats as it flies.

The TURKEY VULTURE, *Cathartes aura* (27-32), in several subspecies ranges over the entire temperate and tropical parts of the New World. The northern-breeding birds retreat southward in winter to the southern part of their range.

The vultures, as an adaptation to their carrion-feeding habits, differ from the other members of the order in having a longer bill with a long cere, turkey-like feet with blunt claws, no shield over the eye, and the head and upper neck bare of feathers.

TURKEY VULTURE (FLYING)

RED-SHOULDERED HAWK
ADULT

SWALLOW-TAILED KITE (FLYING)

IMMATURE

MARSH HAWK
FEMALE   MALE

Scale of foreground figures about one-sixth

PLATE 14

BIRD HAWKS (Family *Accipitridae*)

The three species of hawks assembled on this plate live so largely on birds that they have earned for themselves the name "Bird Hawks." They are common birds, and without doubt it is their extensive destruction of bird life, both wild and domesticated, that has brought the entire hawk tribe into bad repute. If it were possible for the farmer and sportsman to recognize these birds among other hawks their destruction in reasonable numbers would probably not result in any great harm. But the difficulty of distinguishing them from hawks in general results in the slaughter of all hawks. Perhaps the study of the plates here presented may assist in making the desired distinction. Without question, under primitive conditions the role of predators was to assist in maintaining nature's proper balance by reducing the high populations of the most prolific species, but, with the greatly altered relations consequent upon the advent of man, limited local control may be necessary. The hawks here shown have short, stout bills, which are neither toothed nor notched; the wings are short, the tails long. They are swift and dashing in flight, agile and quick in turning and twisting when in pursuit of their prey. The adults are grayish-blue on the backs. This coloring and their impetuous, darting flight have given them the name "Blue Darters." These hawks nest in trees and build bulky nests of sticks easily mistaken for crow's nests. The young are covered with white down.

The COOPER's HAWK, *Accipiter cooperii* (14-20), breeds in southern Canada and south to the southern border of the United States and to northern Mexico; it winters from the northern United States to Costa Rica. Though they all feed to some extent on small mammals, insects, and reptiles, these form but a comparatively small portion of the total food. Cooper's Hawk deserves, more than any other, the name of "Hen Hawk" or "Chicken Hawk." Poultry and game birds make up over a quarter of its food, and various small ground birds a good half of the remainder. The rounded tail of Cooper's Hawk and the square tail of the Sharp-shinned may serve as distinguishing field marks.

The SHARP-SHINNED HAWK, *Accipiter striatus* (10-14), breeds throughout nearly all of Canada and the United States and in northern Mexico; it winters from southeastern Alaska in the west and central New England in the east south to Costa Rica and the West Indies. The Sharp-shinned Hawk, or Little Blue Darter, is not a common bird in the upper Mississippi Valley except during migration, most of them passing farther north to nest. Although at times it strikes its prey on the wing in the open, it more commonly searches through sparse woodlands and about the borders of thickets and hedgerows, ready to pounce with lightning speed upon any startled quarry.

The GOSHAWK of eastern North America, *Accipiter gentilis* (21-25), is one of numerous subspecies widely distributed throughout the Northern Hemisphere. It breeds throughout most of Canada and less commonly in the extreme northern United States; it winters from Alaska through the southern Canadian provinces and much of the United States to northern Mexico. The Goshawk in full adult plumage is a handsome and impressive bird when viewed with unbiased eyes. It is by far the largest of the present trio and is a powerful, bold, rapacious bird. It visits the United States chiefly in winter and feeds largely upon rabbits, but when numerous devours grouse, pheasants, and poultry.

COOPER'S HAWK   SHARP-SHINNED HAWK
        IMMATURE   IMMATURE
ADULT   ADULT

GOSHAWK
                                        ADULT

IMMATURE

Scale about one-sixth

PLATE 15

RED-TAILED HAWK (Family *Accipitridae*)

This plate is devoted mainly to a single species—the RED-TAILED HAWK, *Buteo jamaicensis* (19-25)—for the purpose of bringing into direct contrast several of the very different forms in this confusing complex. The two upper left-hand figures show the adult and young of the typical EASTERN RED-TAIL (*Buteo jamaicensis borealis*), which ranges from the Atlantic seacoast to the Mississippi Valley. It winters chiefly in the southern United States, and in northern Mexico. The upper right-hand figure shows the more rufous WESTERN RED-TAIL (*Buteo jamaicensis calurus*), which is found from western Canada south to Lower California and east to the western border of the Great Plains in the south and to eastern Quebec in the north; it is accidental farther east to the upper Mississippi Valley, including Minnesota; it winters in the Pacific coast region south to Guatemala. The lower left-hand figure is an extreme example of what is known as KRIDER'S HAWK (*Buteo jamaicensis krideri*), usually regarded as a subspecies, but it may be only an example of widespread partial albinism. It occurs in summer in various degrees of whiteness in south central Canada and the north central United States, including the upper Mississippi Valley, and in winter south to the northern Gulf coast. It is frequent in Minnesota, chiefly westward. The lower right-hand figure is the dark, sometimes almost black, HARLAN'S HAWK (*Buteo harlani*), now separated as a species but formerly thought to be a subspecies of the Red-tail. There is much variation from the plumage shown in the specimen in the plate, but the typical *adult* has the "tail freckled, marbled, or mottled with shades of black, white, gray, or red varying in proportion . . . with a tendency to form longitudinal aggregations of specklings" (Taverner). The tail in the young bird is barred and there is interminable variation in the depth of body coloring and markings in the adult. It may be an example of widespread partial melanism, a black or dark color phase not uncommon in other species of hawks. Harlan's breeds in southwestern Alaska and portions of northwestern Canada, and migrates to and from the Gulf states through the Mississippi Valley, when it mingles with other Red-tails. It should, perhaps, be added that this is not the whole story, as there is much difference of opinion among ornithologists as to the real status of the subspecies and color phases of this very variable hawk.

In the northern United States the large hawk seen commonly in the summer months, sailing around slowly on set wings high in the air, is the Red-tail. Other summer hawks, as the Broad-wing and Marsh Hawk, soar also, but they are smaller and less frequently seen high in the air. A high-soaring hawk in the winter is almost certainly an American Rough-leg. The adult Red-tail can always be recognized by the bright reddish-chestnut of the upper surface of the tail when the bird turns or dips in such a way as to bring the upper parts into view. The tail is carried fully expanded, like an open fan, so it shows to good advantage.

The Red-tail is rather slow in flight and not very agile. Considerably more than half of its food consists of mammals, such as gophers, ground squirrels, rabbits, mice, and rats, with the addition of snakes, frogs, and many large insects including a goodly number of grasshoppers. "Where rodents are a serious economic problem, the Red-tailed Hawk is too valuable to be destroyed except under severe provocation" (Taverner).

EASTERN RED-TAILED HAWK   WESTERN RED-TAILED HAWK
ADULT   ADULT
IMMATURE
KRIDER'S RED-TAILED HAWK   HARLAN'S HAWK
ADULT   ADULT

Scale about one-sixth

PLATE 16

HAWKS (Family *Accipitridae*)

The four kinds of hawks shown in this illustration are among the most beneficial of their tribe. Their food consists so largely of harmful rodent animals and injurious insects that they play a most important part in protecting the crops of the agriculturist and horticulturist. Wild birds make up a very negligible part of their food and poultry is even more rarely taken. Swainson's Hawk has been called the Grasshopper Hawk because these pests form such a very large part of its diet, and the Ferruginous Hawk has earned for itself the appellation of Gopher or Ground-squirrel Hawk for the reason that it preys so largely on these highly injurious rodents. That these species have been included in the general massacre of hawks has been a very serious mistake.

They are all hawks of rather slow, seemingly laborious flight and hunt for their quarry by patrolling back and forth at no great height above the earth or by watching from some lowly perch. But at other times, when the fancy moves them, they mount in spirals high in the air and soar lightly and gracefully around in wide circles, silhouetted against the heavens, in the manner of the Red-tail.

These four hawks, like the Red-tail, have a dark-plumage phase in which the normal markings are largely lost. A black hawk seen in the winter is almost certainly a Rough-legged Hawk, but during migration may be a Rough-legged Hawk, the dark phase of the Red-tail, Swainson's, the Ferruginous Hawk, or, rarest of all and much less in size, a melanistic Broad-wing.

The BROAD-WINGED HAWK, *Buteo platypterus* (13.25-18), is an American species breeding in North America east from Alberta and the Great Plains, and wintering from the southern United States to northern South America. Several West Indies races are recognized. The Broad-winged Hawk is the common hawk of the woodlands, as the Marsh Hawk is of the open country. During migration both spring and fall it assembles in immense flocks, and the appearance of these great aggregations excites the farmers and sportsmen and gives rise to the belief that hawks are still enormously abundant. Economically it is a harmless species and its presence in large numbers is a decided advantage rather than an injury to man's interests. It nests in secluded places in the forest and rarely visits farmyards in search of food.

SWAINSON'S HAWK, *Buteo swainsoni* (19.50-22), breeds throughout most of western North America and migrates through Central America to its winter home in Chile. It is preeminently a bird of the prairies and plains, and is but a straggler in wooded areas. Its food habits are such as to place it in the foremost rank of beneficial birds. It is gentle and unsuspicious in nature compared with others of its kind.

The ROUGH-LEGGED HAWK, *Buteo lagopus s. johannis* (19.50-23.50), breeds in Canada, chiefly far north, and winters in the United States. There are closely related representatives in Europe and Asia. This hawk is the large, soaring hawk seen in the winter where the Red-tail is absent. It may be known from the Goshawk, another winter visitant, by its longer wings, darker color, and the presence of a white patch at the base of the tail.

The FERRUGINOUS HAWK or the FERRUGINOUS ROUGH-LEG, *Buteo regalis* (22.50-25), is a bird of western North America, breeding in southern Canada and the western United States, and wintering south to northern Mexico. It lives mainly on the western plains and enters the upper Mississippi Valley in only limited numbers, chiefly in migration. Both this and the Rough-leg are large, handsome birds and worthy of full protection as friends of the farmer and rancher.

BROAD-WINGED HAWK
IMMATURE
ADULT

SWAINSON'S HAWK
IMMATURE
ADULT

FERRUGINOUS HAWK
ADULT

ROUGH-LEGGED HAWK
ADULT

Scale about one-sixth

PLATE 17

EAGLES AND OSPREY (Family *Accipitridae*)

"Once upon a time" the Bald Eagle was common enough in the northern United States so that its immense aerie was to be seen high up in a tall tree beside most of the larger bodies of water and principal streams. As late as seventy-five years ago the sight of one of these great white-headed, white-tailed birds flying over high in the air in spring and fall—for they retreated to the south when the waters froze over—was a not infrequent sight. But today the aeries are few in number and the big birds are objects of special interest.

The other eagle of this region, the Golden Eagle, was probably never very numerous, coming as a winter visitant from farther north and west and remaining only during the colder months. Some of those that came were either wantonly shot or lost their lives while attempting to take the bait from traps set for fur-bearing animals. Today it is an uncommon bird.

The other bird in the illustration is the Osprey, or Fish Hawk, which also has decreased greatly in numbers in the interior of the United States, but there are still infrequent pairs nesting about the larger and more remote lakes.

The BALD EAGLE, *Haliaeetus leucocephalus* (30-43), is a North American bird, with a range extending from Alaska and northern Canada to central Mexico. The more northern-breeding birds are somewhat larger than those breeding in the southern United States and are separated as a subspecies—the Northern Bald Eagle (*H. l. alascanus*)—as distinguished from the Southern Bald Eagle (*H. l. leucocephalus*).

This great bird, sometimes called the Bird of Washington, was chosen by Congress on June 20, 1782, as the national emblem of the United States. When poised proudly on the summit of some towering pinnacle or when soaring majestically and gracefully high in the zenith it is a handsome and commanding figure. In the interior its food consists largely of fish which it picks up dead from the shores of lakes and streams or steals from the more capable fisherman, the Osprey. It may capture disabled mammals or birds and on the seacoasts is said to prey on ducks and other waterfowl. The sexes are alike in color. It ordinarily takes the young bird three years to get the white head and tail.

The GOLDEN EAGLE, *Aquila chrysaëtos* (30-40), is found throughout the Northern Hemisphere. The North American bird (*A. c. canadensis*) breeds in the mountains of northern Alaska and northern Canada, east to Ungava, and south to central Mexico; in winter it is found south as far as the Gulf coast. The Golden Eagle is the finest and noblest of the birds of prey that occur in the interior of North America. The North American Indians used its feathers in making their war and display regalia, admiring it as a courageous and valiant bird. The young Golden Eagle in flight shows a distinct white patch on the outer front part of the wing, which is lacking in the young Bald Eagle. The leg is feathered to the toes in the Golden Eagle, but the lower part of the shank is bare in the Bald Eagle.

The OSPREY or FISH HAWK, *Pandion haliaëtus* (20.75-25), occurs throughout the world in one or another of several subspecies. The North American race (*P. h. carolinensis*) breeds in Alaska and northern Canada, south through the United States to the Gulf and northern Mexico; it winters in the southern United States, the West Indies, Mexico, and Central America, casually to South America.

The flight of the Osprey when looking for its finny prey is slow with occasional periods of sailing at some distance above the water. When it sights a fish it pauses for a moment, then, on set wings, it plunges swiftly with such force that it disappears in a great mass of spray that is thrown up all around it. The nest is a huge affair of sticks, placed in the top of a tall, dead tree and visible for miles around.

GOLDEN EAGLE, ADULT   OSPREY, ADULT

BALD EAGLE

IMMATURE

ADULT

Scale of foreground figures about one-sixth

PLATE 18

FALCONS (Family *Falconidae*)

The true falcons have the upper mandible distinctly toothed and notched near the end of the sharply hooked bill, and the lower mandible with a notch near the squared tip; the wings are long, pointed, and triangular in outline; the nostril is near the base of the bill, round instead of oval, and with a central bony core or tubercle; the shield over the eye is well developed; the legs are short and strong, the toes armed with much-curved, very sharp talons. They are noted for their courage and swift, dashing flight. "They capture their quarry with sudden and violent onslaught, and exhibit raptorial nature in its highest degree" (Coues). There are about sixty species and many subspecies widely distributed throughout the world.

The GYRFALCONS, *Falco rusticolus* (21-24), are large, powerful birds of the arctic regions, circumpolar in distribution and rarely coming south into the United States; they are more frequent along the seacoasts than in the interior. The handsome white bird shown in the plate is the lightest color phase of this species, a very rare straggler into the northern United States, the gray or black phase being the bird that usually appears, and that very infrequently. The Gyrfalcons, the noblest of the many kinds of falcons, were trained, though less commonly than the Peregrine Falcon, and used in the practice of falconry when the royal personages of Europe amused themselves with this sport.

The PRAIRIE FALCON, *Falco mexicanus* (17-20), is a bird of the Great Plains of western North America from southern Canada south to southern Mexico; it breeds from southern Canada to Texas and east as far as the western Dakotas. It enters the prairie portions of the upper Mississippi Valley as a migrant and occurs occasionally in winter. "The Prairie Falcon is the prairie and desert representative of the Peregrine and resembles that species in many ways. It has the same dash and gallant hardihood, but shows more inclination to prey on small mammals, instead of birds" (Taverner).

The PEREGRINE FALCON or DUCK HAWK, *Falco peregrinus* (15.50-20), is a bird of many subspecies, dispersed widely throughout the world. The form occurring over most of North America (*F. p. anatum*) breeds locally in the arctic regions from Alaska to Greenland and south to the southwestern United States and central Mexico in the west, and to the middle states in the east; in winter it is found as far south as the West Indies and Panama and casually to South America. In the upper Mississippi Valley it still nests on cliffs bordering large lakes and streams, but nowhere commonly; it is more often seen in migration. There is very little difference between the American Duck Hawk and the Peregrine Falcon of the Old World.

That the Duck Hawk is nowhere a common bird is perhaps fortunate, as it is one of the most destructive of the birds of prey, living and feeding its young almost entirely upon birds ranging in size from a tiny warbler or swallow to waterfowl the size of a Mallard Duck. Its usual method of hunting is to rise some distance above its prey and then, with a lightning-like plunge, seize it in flight either with talons or beak, or, by delivering a powerful blow with the breast, knock it to earth lifeless. In direct pursuit its flight is so swift that it can easily overtake and seize such rapid-flying birds as pigeons, swifts, and ducks. At the finish it rises above the bird and descends upon it by a quick, downward dart. This dweller on cliffs and crags of the wilderness sometimes sees in the towers and lofty buildings of crowded cities a resemblance to its native haunts, and occasional birds take up a winter residence amid such strange surroundings, preying on the tame pigeons already in possession. It is related that at the inauguration of President Hoover a Duck Hawk viewed the parade from various points along Pennsylvania Avenue.

PEREGRINE FALCON
IMMATURE (FLYING)

PRAIRIE FALCON, ADULT   ADULT

GYRFALCON

Scale of foreground figures about one-sixth

PLATE 19

FALCONS (Family *Falconidae*)

The two attractively colored hawks in this plate are the smallest of the North American falcons. The Pigeon Hawk, a trifle larger than the Sparrow Hawk, maintains the reputation of the true falcons in being, like them, a bird-killer, and were it not a rather uncommon bird it would, despite its small size, be a serious menace to bird life, for it is capable of capturing not only small birds but prey as large as poultry, tame pigeons, and waterfowl. This fault, so far as man's interests are concerned, is offset to some extent by the fact that it includes in its diet a considerable number of injurious insects and small mammals. The Sparrow Hawk feeds chiefly on insects, mice, ground squirrels, and other small mammals. Birds enter but sparingly into its food except when it is feeding its young. It deserves to be classed as generally beneficial, for the good services it renders much more than compensate for any undesirable traits. It has, unfortunately, been included in the present general destruction of hawks and is now greatly reduced in numbers in most settled regions.

The PIGEON HAWK, *Falco columbarius* (10-13.25), ranges throughout the Northern Hemisphere in a number of subspecies. The bird of eastern North America is the Eastern Pigeon Hawk (*F. c. columbarius*), which breeds in eastern Canada and the adjacent parts of the United States west to Manitoba and the eastern border of the Great Plains. It winters from the Gulf states south through eastern Mexico to northern South America, and in the West Indies. The American Pigeon Hawks are the New World representatives of the Merlins of the Old World. The Pigeon Hawk is in many ways a diminutive Duck Hawk but in its manner of hunting it is more like the Sharp-shinned Hawk, prowling through woodlands and about the borders of thickets and hedgerows. It may nest in a hole like the Sparrow Hawk but more commonly in an open nest among the branches of a tree or on a ledge of a cliff. The name Pigeon Hawk may have come from its striking resemblance, both in flight and at rest, to the extinct Passenger Pigeon, but it has also been suggested that it may have preyed upon pigeons to such an extent as to merit the name.

The SPARROW HAWK, *Falco sparverius* (8.75-12), is a wide-ranging bird of the Americas, found in North, Central, and South America and the outlying islands. The race found over most of North America is the EASTERN SPARROW HAWK (*F. s. sparverius*), which breeds from tree-limit entirely across northern Canada, south to the northwestern United States and farther east to eastern Texas and the Gulf states (except Florida and the immediate Gulf coast west to Alabama). It winters chiefly in the southern United States, south through eastern Mexico to Panama. The Sparrow Hawk is a close relative of the European Kestrel or Windhover. This handsome little hawk is unlike most of its kind in that the male and female are of nearly the same size and differ markedly in plumage, as is shown in the illustration. The young, too, immediately on shedding their fluffy white down assume the garbs of their respective parents. Thus male and female differ from the very start. The Sparrow Hawk nests in a hole in a tree or other cavity, even a nesting box at times. Its method of hunting is to winnow slowly back and forth over open ground, pausing suddenly now and then, perhaps backing up a foot or so to remain poised on forward-beating wings and expanded drooping tail, and then in a quick downward dive to seize the quarry that has been discovered in the tangled grass—most frequently a large grasshopper, often a mouse, rarely a small bird. The fact that it captures many dragonflies shows that it can be quick and agile in action.

PIGEON HAWK

FEMALE   MALE

SPARROW HAWK

                                                     FEMALE

MALE

Scale about one-sixth

PLATE 20

GROUSE (Family *Tetraonidae*)

This is a small group of fowl-like birds, the grouse of the world numbering only eighteen species scattered throughout the Northern Hemisphere. Like the other gallinaceous birds, chickens, quail, turkeys, and their relatives, the grouse have short, strong bills, with the upper mandible closing over the lower, and with stout legs and feet. Grouse differ from the other gallinaceous birds in having feathered tarsi; ptarmigan, members of the grouse family, have completely feathered toes. Some grouse spend considerable time in trees feeding on buds and berries, although others are inhabitants of the tundra, prairies, and sage areas and are rarely found in trees. The sexes are similar in plumage, although some, such as the Spruce Grouse, differ greatly. Male grouse usually have a bare area over the eye which in the breeding season becomes enlarged and brilliantly colored, and some species have fleshy pouches that are inflated and used in sexual displays in the breeding season. In many species the cocks have elaborate mating performances. The nest is on the ground, the eggs numerous; the downy young leave the nest at once and are cared for by the hen.

The SPRUCE GROUSE, *Canachites canadensis* (15-16.50), is an inhabitant of the evergreen forests of northern North America. Of the several subspecies, the one occurring in southern Canada east from Manitoba and the adjacent parts of the United States is *C. c. canace*. It is a permanent resident where found and was once common in suitable localities in the northern United States but is now greatly reduced in numbers. It is often called the Spruce Partridge, Spruce Hen, or Fool Hen, the latter name because of its excessive tameness, which contributed to its disappearance. It is typically a bird of dense, dark, wet, spruce-tamarack-white-cedar swamps but may also be found not infrequently on the upland. It is not a very desirable game bird as the flesh is dark and usually tastes of the spruce needles on which it feeds so largely.

The courting performance of the Spruce cock is enacted in a small open space in the forest, and consists of repeated flights to and fro between established perches at either end of the area, the bird alighting on the ground each time and rising vertically with a whirring of the wings, audible for only a short distance. There is nothing to compare with the loud "drumming" of the Ruffed Grouse. In addition to these aerial activities there is a marvelous strutting display in which all the varied plumage is shown off to full advantage in the manner of a little turkey cock.

The RUFFED GROUSE, *Bonasa umbellus* (17.12-18.25), more commonly called Partridge or "Patridge" by sportsmen, occurs in several subspecies throughout the more northern woodlands of North America. It is a permanent resident where found. One of the most interesting things about the Ruffed Grouse is the so-called "drumming" of the male bird. To the uninitiated it is one of the most mysterious and puzzling sounds of the forest. It may be mistaken for low, distant thunder or a faraway rumbling of unaccountable origin. It is produced by the beating of the air with the wings, at first slow and measured, increasing to a rapid whir. The cock also struts before the hen, in mating time, exhibiting to perfection his glorious fan-shaped tail and splendid black neck ruffs.

This grouse is unquestionably, from every point of view, the finest upland game bird in North America. If hunted in true sportsman-like fashion, it provides a very special test of skill and as a table bird it certainly has no equal, the flesh being white and tender and with a delicious flavor all its own.

SPRUCE GROUSE

FEMALE   MALE

RUFFED GROUSE

RED PHASE

GRAY PHASE

Scale about one-fourth

PLATE 21

PRAIRIE CHICKEN (Family *Tetraonidae*)

The GREATER PRAIRIE CHICKEN or PINNATED GROUSE, *Tympanuchus cupido* (16.75-17.75), is, or was, an inhabitant of the plains and prairies of North America east of the Rocky Mountains from southern Canada south to the Mexican border. Under the name Heath Hen (*T. c. cupido*) it was in early days common in the north and central Atlantic states but is now extinct there. The birds of a portion of the Gulf coast are regarded as a subspecies, Attwater's Prairie Chicken (*T. c. attwateri*). The birds of the southwestern Great Plains are a distinct species, the Lesser Prairie Chicken (*T. pallidicinctus*).

The early history of the Prairie Hen, or Pinnated Grouse, west of the Alleghany Mountains, shows clearly that it extended its original range westward and northwestward just as the country was settled, keeping pace with the forefront of the grainfields. There were no Pinnated Grouse in that region in the days of the early explorers. Their "Prairie Chickens" were Sharp-tailed Grouse. The Pinnated came with the settlers who broke the prairie soil and planted crops at various times during the early half of the nineteenth century. It increased rapidly, as is its wont when little disturbed, and by the middle of the century had become abundant over most of this reclaimed area, the native Sharp-tail growing scarcer as it retreated westward and northward. Instead of being a wild, unadaptable bird that will not and cannot live in contact with civilization, as is frequently argued, it is exactly the opposite. Farming conditions and forest clearings are what brought it into the region and amid such surroundings it is at home and thrives. If left to itself for a long period of time or indefinitely, as some think should be done, it would in all probability multiply greatly and become once more a common bird, regardless of settled conditions. The experiment is surely worth trying, but it can only be done with a change of heart and the cooperation of those who, at present, insist that they shall be permitted periodically to take toll from its thinning ranks the moment that it shows signs of recovery. Propagation for restocking has never been successful; saving the wild birds is the only way.

The spring "booming" or "tooting" of the Prairie Chicken, associated with its courting display or so-called "dance," is one of the most interesting and striking episodes in its life history. The cocks assemble at break of day on a knoll on the prairie or in a meadow, with or without the presence of hens, and soon thereafter the performance begins. Each cock has his own chosen spot and here he puffs out his feathers, flicks his tail, lowers his wings and head, swings the long feathers on the sides of his neck forward and upward, stamps rapidly and vigorously with his feet, inflates two big, bare, orange-colored sacs on the sides of the neck, and emits a deep-toned, far-carrying, three-syllabled "boom," which has been likened to the words "old-mul-doon." There is much dashing rapidly about, springing into the air, loud cackling, and real or pretended encounters between neighboring cocks, but no orderly, formal dancing as has been described by some authors. For several hours this goes on and the whole scene is an animated and, to the onlooker, an amusing one. The two sacs are really one large sac produced by the inflation of the modified upper part of the gullet; it acts as a reverberator or drum to increase the volume of the sound that is produced in the voice box at the lower end of the windpipe. It is not connected with the lungs or air sacs of the body as formerly supposed.

It will be noticed in the plate that the legs of the adult bird, there shown, are fully feathered to the toes. In the young birds of the year the legs are yellow and nearly bare of feathers, which has led some sportsmen to believe that there are two kinds of Prairie Chicken—a bare-legged and a feather-legged variety.

PLATE 21

GREATER PRAIRIE CHICKEN OR PINNATED GROUSE

FEMALE   MALE IN DISPLAY

Scale about one-fourth

PLATE 22

SHARP-TAILED GROUSE (Family *Tetraonidae*)

The SHARP-TAILED GROUSE, *Pedioecetes phasianellus* (18-20), was formerly an inhabitant of much of the prairie country, brushland, and open woodlands of the interior and western parts of North America. Its range has been considerably curtailed in recent years. Several races are recognized. It is resident where found.

This grouse is known among hunters by a variety of common names more or less descriptive of its appearance or habits. The most common, perhaps, are Pintail Grouse, Spike-tail, White-breasted Grouse, and Brush Grouse; sometimes simply "Grouse" as distinguishing it from the Prairie Chicken. It is less of a prairie bird than the latter species, preferring brushlands and open areas in forests.

When the region comprising the extreme upper portion of the Mississippi Valley and the adjacent parts of Canada was an unsettled wilderness, the Prairie Sharp-tailed Grouse was the "Chicken" of all that territory. When travelers into these parts, previous to the early part of the nineteenth century, made reference to Prairie Hens or Chickens it was the Sharp-tail they saw, as there were no Pinnated there at that time. With the advance of settlements and the planting of grainfields the Sharp-tail retreated to the west and north and the Pinnated or Prairie Chicken came in from the southeast and east to take its place. The Sharp-tail is by nature a wilder bird than the Prairie Chicken and does not adapt itself so readily to civilized conditions. The virgin prairie was its home in the summer and natural woodlands in the fall and winter. The Sharp-tail, especially in the winter, is more of a tree-browsing bird than the Pinnated.

The Sharp-tail is similar in habits in many ways to the Prairie Chicken, but being so largely a bird of the woods it roosts more commonly at night in trees. It may at times burrow in the snow in the manner of the Ruffed Grouse and Prairie Chicken. Like the latter bird it assembles in the fall in flocks or "packs" and so passes the winter. These packs may be composed of all cocks or all hens. The "hen-packs" do not wander southward in search of better feeding grounds as do those of the Prairie Chicken, the fall and spring flights of which, to and from the cornfields of Iowa, simulate a migratory movement.

The male Sharp-tailed Grouse, like the Pinnated, has a spring courting and mating "dance" with accompanying vocal utterances. It is, also, an early morning performance and is staged under like conditions. The cock in full display is shown in the illustration, drawn and colored by Mr. Jaques from photographs and color studies made in the field by Mr. Breckenridge. There are no long neck plumes to be manipulated as in the Pinnated, the sacs are purple instead of orange and are smaller, the drooping wings are raised from the body, and the brilliant white under tail-coverts and two long middle tail feathers are used to advantage. The strutting cock, usually facing another cock similarly engaged, lowers his head, inflates the sacs, rustles the wing and tail feathers, utters a medley of cackles, gobbles, and coos, and moves and turns about like a mechanical toy on rapidly stamping feet. On the instant, as at a signal, all the performing birds stop suddenly, become still and rigid, to begin again in a few seconds all together. At intervals all the cocks dash about the field in full display, stopping and freezing in exact unison, and then, as one bird, continuing the frenzied race. Altogether it is a more weird and grotesque "dance" than that of the Pinnated Grouse. Mr. Seton likened it to a Cree Indian dance and suggested that it may have provided the Indians with the motive for their performance.

PLATE 22

SHARP-TAILED GROUSE

Scale about one-fourth

MALE IN DISPLAY

FEMALES

PLATE 23

BOBWHITE QUAIL (Family *Phasianidae*)

The pheasants, partridges, and quail (family *Phasianidae*), a group widely distributed in the world, are separated from the grouse (family *Tetraonidae*) by their unfeathered instead of feathered shanks, feet, and nostrils. The Old World partridges and pheasants differ structurally very little from the American quails. The Bobwhite is the only native representative of the group in eastern North America, but there are several other quail farther west, some of them very attractive birds with crests and head plumes.

The BOBWHITE, or BOBWHITE QUAIL, *Colinus virginianus,* is a widely distributed species in eastern United States, ranging west to North Dakota and eastern New Mexico and south to Guatemala. Throughout this large range the Bobwhite varies greatly in coloration and other adaptations to diverse climates and habitats. Birds transplanted from one region to another by well-intentioned sportsman groups and game departments have done little to increase the Bobwhite, and through the interbreeding of several races may have weakened populations adapted to local conditions. The Bobwhite is a permanent resident where found. Its attempts to establish itself west and north of southeastern Minnesota have not met with much success and early records seem to indicate that it is a comparatively recent comer into all this region. The various explorers into this country in the early part of the nineteenth century (Pike, Keating of the Long Expedition, Schoolcraft, Featherstonhaugh, and others), though they make frequent mention of both game and non-game birds never mention the quail. If present it was evidently very rare.

Everyone knows the clear, ringing, far-carrying whistle of the male Bobwhite, uttered with rising inflection and variously interpreted as *bob-white, ah-bob-white, wha-whoi, wha-wha-whoi, buck-wheat-ripe, more-wet, more-more-wet, more-wheat,* etc., etc. It attracts the attention and is the delight of old and young alike. It is said that this call is usually given only by unmated males. The Bobwhite, when unmolested, is a gentle, friendly creature, coming confidingly about farms and dwellings and into the environs of cities and towns. It builds its nest beside the path or in the fence corner and not infrequently in the shrubbery of city yards and parks. The nest is usually well concealed in long, dense grass, which is drawn together above to form a protecting canopy. The eggs are numerous—twelve to eighteen—short, pear-shaped, and plain white in color. The young leave the nest as soon as they are hatched, keeping together and being led by one or both parents. As soon as they are too large to be brooded at night (at about three weeks), they gather close together in a compact, circular formation, heads out and tails in, which affords both warmth and defense against enemies, there being no possibility of a rear attack. The fact that the birds, when suddenly startled under such conditions, burst upward and outward in all directions has given rise to the name "bomb formation."

The quail of a covey, when flushed, rise together with a loud whirring of wings and fly rapidly at no great height, with alternating short periods of rapid wing-beats and of sailing on down-curved, set wings. They may alight all together or somewhat scattered. When forced to fly a second time they usually separate and alight some distance apart. Then after a few minutes may be heard the "gathering," "scatter," or "covey" call, a shrill *ke-loi-kee? ka-loi-kee?* answered by a *whoil-kee,* by means of which the scattered birds get together again.

PLATE 23

BOBWHITE OR BOBWHITE QUAIL

MALES: WHITE FACE   FEMALES: BUFFY FACE

Scale of foreground figures about one-eighth

PLATE 24

GROUSE AND BOBWHITE QUAIL CHICKS

This attractive illustration is designed to show the pretty plumage of the chicks of certain of the North American grouse and of the Bobwhite. The little Bobwhite Quail at the top was not long from the egg but, although it is here shown resting on its whole feet, it is really able, even at this tender age, to get up and run about nimbly, if a bit unsteadily, at the call of the parent. There are usually twelve or fourteen, sometimes more, of these little puffballs in a family party and almost immediately after they are free from the shell they leave the nest, to be cared for by one or both parents. Should the youngsters stray away they may join another brood or may be adopted and cared for by an unmated cock. In one-third of the nests studied by Stoddard in Georgia the cock incubated the eggs, brought off the young, and cared for them in the absence or death of the female. The wings grow rapidly while the body is still largely covered with down, and at about three weeks the young flush with the parents. At the end of about four weeks the body down has given place to the juvenal feathers, but the head and neck are still downy for some time longer. At two months the chicks are half-grown and in another six weeks may weigh as much as the old birds and closely resemble them in plumage (Stoddard).

The four grouse chicks are farther advanced than the little quail. The wings are well grown, and in the Ruffed Grouse and Sharp-tail the body plumage is appearing, though the heads and necks in all are still downy. This series of chicks serves to show plainly the order of appearance of the juvenal plumage. The early development of the wings and the power of flight in these terrestrial birds is a great advantage in the face of many dangers that beset them on all sides. To this ability to escape by flight is added another and greater asset in the concealing character of the plumage, together with an inherent instinct to lie close and motionless when danger threatens. All these little grouse and the young Bobwhite are adept at what is termed "freezing." At a word, or rather a cluck, from the parent each little chick instantly flattens itself on the ground beside or beneath a dead leaf, a twig, or a wisp of dry grass, and presto! immediately it disappears as if by magic. Nothing is alive except its tiny, watchful eye and nothing will induce it to move until there comes a reassuring note from the guarding parent. It is almost unbelievable how perfect is the concealment. Hunt as one may there is apparently nothing there, right where a moment before were a dozen or more of these elusive little creatures. Should a chick by chance be discovered it will as likely as not be right on a spot repeatedly examined before. During the first weeks of life, when this ruse is most effective, it must puzzle many a wild prowler in search of a meal, but should the little hider be discovered it only makes the resulting tragedy the more certain. As the birds grow older it is more and more difficult for them to conceal themselves by squatting and the mortality among them from prowling and flying predators is considerable. From the time the young are about half-grown, when disturbed by a barking dog an entire covey will flush together into the trees above and there "freeze" and remain rigidly stationary until the danger is past, however long it may be.

The new feathers on the back of the four little grouse in the illustration present a beautiful array of markings. The broad, white stripe down the middle of each feather, bordered narrowly by black and widening abruptly at the tip, is most striking and effective. When the feathers are in perfect position the result is a series of wide, white stripes, crossed at intervals by white bars and relieved throughout by a narrow black border—a pretty pattern common to all the grouse at this stage and carried to some extent into succeeding plumages in most species. Later the feathers may split at the ends, forming a notch bordered with white.

BOBWHITE, DOWNY CHICK

GROUSE CHICKS, JUVENAL PLUMAGE DEVELOPING

RUFFED GROUSE   SPRUCE GROUSE
GREATER PRAIRIE CHICKEN   SHARP-TAILED GROUSE

Scale about three-fourths

PLATE 25

RING-NECKED PHEASANT AND
GRAY PARTRIDGE (Family *Phasianidae*)

The two game birds shown in this plate have been introduced into North America from the Old World but both, especially the Ring-necked Pheasant, have become so well established in certain regions that they are now an integral part of our bird life and have to be so considered.

Pheasants (Family *Phasianidae*) are natives of Asia but have been so widely dispersed by the transplanting of various species and races that now one or more representatives may be found in almost all parts of the world. William Beebe in his *Monograph of the Pheasants* describes sixty species and many subspecies. They are generally large birds, the cocks adorned with much lengthened, brilliantly colored feathers; the head partly or wholly bare and brightly colored, with comb or wattles; the legs bare of feathers and frequently with spurs. The hens are plain. The cock usually has more than one mate. Domestic chickens are descended from pheasant ancestors.

The RING-NECKED PHEASANT, *Phasianus colchicus* (20.50-36), is known in this country by a variety of common names: English Pheasant, Mongolian Pheasant, and Chinese Pheasant. It is largely a composite, produced by the interbreeding of several races, dominant among them being the Eastern Chinese Pheasant, which has imposed its characters to the extent of establishing the white neck ring (absent in several races), so conspicuous a feature of the American cock bird. It is stated that the earliest importation of pheasants into North America was late in the eighteenth century, by a son-in-law of Benjamin Franklin. These birds were from England and were probably the "English Black-neck" race. They were liberated in New Jersey. This and subsequent early attempts were unsuccessful, the birds failing to establish themselves. Since the middle of the nineteenth century successful importations from both Europe and Asia into all parts of the United States and southern Canada have resulted in the birds becoming so abundant that annual kills of many thousands in a single state are possible without serious effect on the breeding stock. In more recent years breeding and stocking have taken the place of importation.

The Ring-necked Pheasant thrives best in an open, farming country where the climate is not too severe and snow not too deep or lasting. It roosts commonly on the ground but may resort to trees at times, especially to escape night-prowling enemies. It is usually, but not always, polygamous, and a cock may have a harem of half a dozen or more hens. Where the pheasant is abundant there has been considerable complaint of its depredations upon garden and field crops. This is true locally, but it has been shown that its summer food contains a very large proportion of insects, many of which are injurious species. This, together with the fact that it now provides the greater part of upland game shooting, should more than balance the harm that it may do. The cock is a gorgeous bird and now that it is here it is to be hoped that it will always survive in large enough numbers to adorn the countryside and delight the admiring wayfarer.

The GRAY or HUNGARIAN PARTRIDGE, *Perdix perdix* (12-14), is an Old World bird that was first introduced into North America by the same son-in-law of Benjamin Franklin who brought over the pheasant. This and other importations into the Atlantic coast states failed and have continued to fail east of the Alleghanies until the present time in spite of the fact that many thousands of the birds have been liberated there. Northwestward in the United States and in western Canada importations have met with success, and the species is now well established and becoming common in some places. Most, if not all, of the later implantations have come from Czechoslovakia—a hardier race than the English bird.

PLATE 25

RING-NECKED PHEASANT

MALE
FEMALE

MALE

GRAY OR
HUNGARIAN PARTRIDGE

ADULT

Scale about one-fifth

PLATE 26

CRANES (Family *Gruidae*) AND GREAT BLUE HERON (Family *Ardeidae*)

Cranes are large, long-necked, long-legged birds, suggesting herons in general appearance, but the plumage is more compact than in herons, the head is partly bare of feathers, the hind toe is small and elevated; the windpipe is elongated and in the adult is coiled for a part of its length in the keel of the breastbone. Cranes are more terrestrial in habit than herons, nesting on the ground, never in trees as do many of the herons. Their nearest North American allies are the rails, gallinules, and coots. There are fourteen species scattered throughout the world, some of which are elegantly adorned. In early spring, during the mating season, cranes congregate on some prairie eminence and engage in spectacular and fantastic "dances" and at other times rise high in the heavens and disport themselves in graceful and impressive aerial evolutions.

The WHOOPING CRANE, *Grus americana* (49-56), now nearly extinct, formerly bred commonly on the interior plains of Canada from the latitude of Hudson Bay south to Iowa and Nebraska in the United States. In migration it reached the Atlantic coast on the east and the eastern foothills of the Rockies on the west. It wintered from the Gulf states to central Mexico. The few that are left nest in the swampy wilderness of southern Mackenzie and winter in southern Texas. This magnificent bird still nested occasionally in the upper Mississippi Valley as late as 1894 and was probably common there in earlier times. In more recent years, even to the present, transients have been reported occasionally in the eastern Dakotas and still more frequently in Oklahoma. Bent has said of the Whooping Crane that it is "one of the grandest and most striking of North American birds. . . . It has retreated before advancing civilization, farther west and then farther north, for it is one of our wildest birds, it cannot stand human companionship and it loves the great open spaces in primitive solitudes." To this may be added that the disappearance of both the Whooping and Sandhill cranes was due, in part at least, to the fact that they were killed in large numbers as game, for the young birds were said to equal the turkey as a table viand.

The SANDHILL CRANE, *Grus canadensis,* which nests in the north central United States and in southern Canada, is the larger (*G. c. tabida*) of two races found in the north central states. This rare bird now nests only in a few local areas within its breeding range. The smaller race, *G. c. canadensis,* formerly called Little Brown or Lesser Sandhill Crane, nests in arctic Canada and Alaska. It is still found in considerable numbers migrating through the mid-continental prairies to winter in the southern United States and northern Mexico.

The GREAT BLUE HERON, *Ardea herodias* (42-52), in one or another of several races breeds over most of North America; it winters south to Central America, and occasionally reaches northern South America.

The Great Blue Heron was included in this plate for the purpose of direct comparison, as it is so commonly called the "Blue Crane." It is not a crane either in classification or habits, though its general appearance may suggest such a relationship. The distinguishing characters are stated above and in the text with Plate 4. This heron breeds in colonies, usually in the tops of tall trees but sometimes in marshes or on rocky islands and often associated with colonies of other species.

PLATE 26

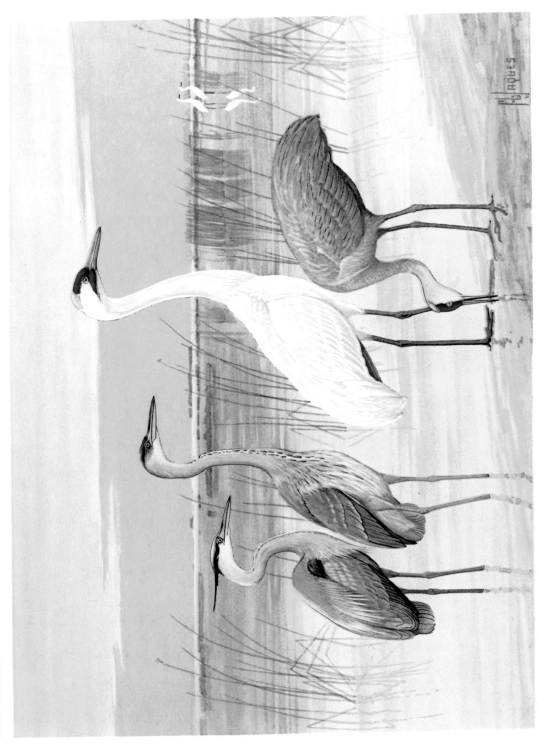

GREAT BLUE HERON
ADULT   IMMATURE

WHOOPING CRANE

SANDHILL CRANE

Scale about one-tenth

PLATE 27

RAILS (Family *Rallidae*)

This is a numerous and important family, widely distributed, and most abundant in the tropics. The North American species all live in marshes and weedy lakes, have large legs and feet and small, short, and rounded wings. They are all noisy birds, the marshes in the spring resounding with their loud, varied, and peculiar calls. They build bulky, usually canopied, nests, supported among the reeds and rushes, and they lay many spotted and usually buff-colored eggs. The rails are mostly plain-colored birds with narrow bodies, the easier to slip about among the marsh vegetation; there are no frontal shields as in the gallinules and coots (Plate 28); they have long, naked toes and short tails, which are usually carried tilted up, and, in walking, both heads and tails are bobbed and flicked in unison with the steps. The coal-black, downy chicks leave the nest as soon as hatched. Rails are skulkers, flush reluctantly, and fly heavily for short distances with dangling legs.

The KING RAIL, *Rallus elegans* (17-19), is much the largest of the species. It breeds from southwestern Ontario and the northern United States east from the Dakotas, south to the Gulf states and, as an allied race, in Cuba; it winters in the southern part of its breeding range. The King Rail is locally a common bird in sloughs and marshes. It utters a variety of notes, prominent among them being a loud, forcible *bup, bup, bup,* increasing in rapidity and the syllables blending toward the end.

The VIRGINIA RAIL, *Rallus limicola* (8.50-10.50), in several closely allied races occurs throughout most of North America and south into South America. The North American race breeds across the continent from southern Canada south to the central United States and locally in northern Mexico; it winters mainly in the southern United States and south through Mexico to Central America. The Virginia Rail, as will be seen in the illustration, is an almost exact reduced replica of the King Rail. The courtship notes have been represented by the syllables *"kid-ick, kid-ick, kid-ick,"* or at times *"cut, cut, cut-ah, cut-ah"* (Townsend).

The SORA, *Porzana carolina* (7.85-9.75), has a very wide distribution, occurring throughout North America, south from southern Canada, and in winter south through the West Indies and Central America to Venezuela and Peru, breeding throughout the northern part of this range.

The Sora is often called the Carolina Rail, Chicken-billed Rail, Rail-bird, and a variety of other names, and is one of the most abundant members of its family. A weak flier though it appears to be in its summer home, it has nevertheless been found in far-away Bermuda, England, Wales, and Scotland. The "song" of the Sora is a descending sequence of clear, whistled notes beginning high and dropping rapidly in both pitch and volume, and usually described as a "whinny."

The YELLOW RAIL, *Coturnicops noveboracensis* (6-7.75), has been found locally in the breeding season over much of North America but there is comparatively little definite information in regard to its nesting. It winters in the Gulf states and north to North Carolina and California. Nests have been found in North Dakota and southern Minnesota and it probably breeds throughout the upper Mississippi Valley.

The Yellow Rail is a pretty little creature, the adult resembling in a general way a small, yellow chicken. Its diminutive size, reluctance to fly, and mouse-like elusiveness amid the dense marsh vegetation where it dwells, make it very difficult to find. Its notes may be represented by the syllables *kuk-kuk—kuk, kuk, kuk,* very like the sound made by driving a tent pin into hard ground.

PLATE 27

SORA
ADULT
CHICKS

IMMATURE, FALL

KING RAIL
ADULT
CHICK

YELLOW RAIL
IMMATURE
ADULT

VIRGINIA RAIL
JUVENAL PLUMAGE   ADULT
CHICK

Scale about one-third

PLATE 28

GALLINULES AND COOTS (Family *Rallidae*)

The gallinules and coots differ from the rails in having a frontal plate or shield extending up from the base of the upper mandible onto the forehead. The bill is short and usually stout. The toes are long and slender in the gallinules, with only a narrow lateral web, if any, but in the coots the toes, including the hind toe, have wide, lobed, lateral membranes, adapted for swimming. The gallinules have rather narrow bodies and loose plumage like the rails, while the coots have flattened bodies and dense plumage like ducks, which they resemble in habits. There are thirty species of gallinules, widely distributed in warm countries, and among them are birds of beautiful, iridescent plumage. Coots number about a dozen species, occurring in various parts of the world; only one species belongs to North America.

The COMMON or FLORIDA GALLINULE, *Gallinula chloropus cachinnans* (12-14.75), breeds across the continent from central California in the west to southern Ontario and Vermont in the east, south to the West Indies, Mexico, and Panama, also in the Galapagos Islands and Bermuda; it is casual farther north. It winters from the southern United States southward. Allied races occur in South America and in the Old World.

On a late spring day in some northern slough, when the new growth is not yet visible, there may be seen a dark, slate-colored bird resembling a coot, picking its way in and out among the broken-down stubble of last year's growth. If, on close examination, it is found that the bill, instead of being white as in the coot, is a conspicuous bright red, then the bird is the Common Gallinule. It is more slender than the coot, walks or wades by preference, swimming only when forced to do so. It bobs its head and flicks its up-turned tail as it moves about, submerged at times to almost the level of the back, and swimming short distances only when its long toes fail to support it on the floating debris. The nest as usually placed is a basket-like structure of reed and grass leaves, lightly canopied, and contains eight to twelve buff-colored spotted and speckled eggs. The nestlings are pretty little black-bodied, red-faced, and almost bald creatures, with absurdly large legs and feet. They can run with ease, supported by the floating and submerged vegetation. The scarlet frontal plate does not appear until the second year. Gallinules are exceedingly noisy birds and their discordant, hen-like cacklings, interspersed with loud and often shrill cries, may be continued all through the night.

The AMERCIAN COOT or MUDHEN, *Fulica americana americana* (13-16.25), is found in North America from southern Canada southward and from the West Indies south through Central America to Panama; it breeds commonly over most of this range except in the eastern United States, where it is largely a migrant. It winters chiefly from the southern United States to the West Indies and Costa Rica and north on the Pacific coast to British Columbia. An allied race occurs in northern South America.

In the spring of the year and again in the fall the coot may be seen alone, in little parties, or in dense flocks in open-water lakes, consorting, it may be, with various species of ducks. The white bill and bobbing head distinguish it. It is a good swimmer and diver but has much difficulty in rising from the surface, finding it necessary to paddle rapidly along with feet and wings splashing vigorously, until it finally gets up enough speed to rise in the air hydroplane-fashion. Once on the wing it flies well, maintaining a direct course, but is not as speedy as a duck. It goes to sloughs and reedy lakes to nest. The eggs are light buff or drab, speckled all over with black or dark brown. The nestlings are gaudy, bizarre little things and are out of the nest soon after being hatched.

PLATE 28

BIRD PORTRAITS IN COLOR

Allan Brooks -
1930.

COMMON GALLINULE   AMERICAN COOT OR MUD-HEN

ADULT   JUVENAL PLUMAGE   CHICKS   ADULT   JUVENAL PLUMAGE

CHICK

Scale of foreground figures about one-fourth

PLATE 29

PLOVERS (Family *Charadriidae*)

The plovers and their allies form one of numerous families assembled in a large order, *Charadriiformes,* which includes such diverse-appearing birds as the jacanas of the American tropics, the oyster-catchers, the shore birds, the gulls and terns, the auks and puffins, etc. Mention of the major subdivisions is omitted, only the families represented in the illustrations being considered here. Plovers are world-wide in distribution but not very numerous in species. They vary in size from large to very small birds. The bill is shorter than the head, more or less swollen at the end and depressed in the middle, pigeon-like. The hind toe is usually absent; if present it is small and elevated. The toes are partly webbed. The shank is covered all around with small, six-sided scales. Plovers are rather more upland birds than are the other shore birds, though some species mingle with the waders on beaches and mud flats.

The PIPING PLOVER, *Charadrius melodus* (6-7.80), is unevenly distributed as a breeding bird from southern Canada, east from Alberta, south to North Carolina and Nebraska. It winters mainly on the coasts of the South Atlantic and Gulf states. The little Piping Plover constructs its simple nest on a sand bar, not far from the water's edge. Its back is the color of dry sand, which makes it difficult to detect when at rest, but serves to distinguish it from its darker-backed relative, the Semipalmated Plover.

The SEMIPALMATED PLOVER, *Charadrius semipalmatus* (6.50-8.05), breeds in the far north and winters from the southern United States to Patagonia and Chile. It is one of the most widely distributed of the shore birds in winter. The Semipalmated Plover is a frequent migrant through the United States and should be looked for on sand bars and mud flats. Its dark back distinguishes it from the Piping Plover, which appears very light in comparison.

The KILLDEER, *Charadrius vociferus* (9-10.50), as a species has one of the most extensive breeding ranges of American Shore Birds. It nests throughout most of Canada, the whole of the United States, the Bahamas, the West Indies, central Mexico, southern Lower California, and the coast of Peru. The resident West Indian and Peruvian birds are separate races. The North American race winters in the southern part of its breeding range and southward to Venezuela and Peru. The Killdeer is a common summer resident throughout most of North America. Its loud and penetrating notes, *kill-dee, kill-dee,* are heard everywhere on upland and lowland alike.

The AMERICAN GOLDEN PLOVER, *Pluvialis dominica dominica* (10-10.62), breeds in the arctic regions, chiefly west of Hudson Bay, and winters on the pampas of Brazil, Argentina, and adjoining countries. Its long fall flight eastward from its breeding grounds to Newfoundland and southward 2400 miles over the Atlantic Ocean to South America is one of the marvels of bird migration. Its return in the spring is by way of western South America, across the Gulf of Mexico, and through the interior of North America. The Golden Plover is one of the many shore birds that suffered in the past from excessive shooting, and now only remnants of the former great flocks remain. It is largely an upland bird.

The BLACK-BELLIED PLOVER, *Squatarola squatarola* (10.50-13.65), is found nearly throughout the world, breeding in the far north, and in the Americas wintering as far south as Brazil, Peru, and Chile, and in the Old World to South Africa, also in India and Australia. The Black-bellied Plover was formerly a common migrant through the United States, but is now much reduced in numbers, having suffered at the hands of gunners as did the Golden Plover. It is more likely to be found on beaches and mud flats than is the latter species.

PLATE 29

BLACK-BELLIED PLOVER   KILLDEER, ADULT

FALL AND WINTER ADULT AND IMMATURE BREEDING ADULT SEMIPALMATED PLOVER, ADULT

AMERICAN GOLDEN PLOVER

FALL AND WINTER ADULT AND IMMATURE BREEDING ADULT PIPING PLOVER, ADULT

Scale of foreground figures about one-third

PLATE 30

WOODCOCKS, SNIPES, AND SANDPIPERS (Family *Scolopacidae*)

This is a large and widely distributed family, and to it belong most of our shore birds. They are like the plovers in some respects, but lack the constriction in the middle of the bill, which is deeply grooved for much of its length; the hind toe is commonly present, though it is absent in the case of the Sanderling. With but few exceptions they are typical waders.

The AMERICAN WOODCOCK, *Philohela minor* (10-12), breeds throughout the eastern United States and southern Canada, west to Manitoba and central Minnesota, and south to the Gulf states; it winters chiefly in the southern United States. The Woodcock has been reduced in numbers in recent years.

The Woodcock trusts for protection to the marvelous dead-leaf and dried-grass pattern of its plumage and flushes only when close-pressed, darting away on whirring wings in a zigzag course through the brush and trees. The incubating bird crouches low and leaves the nest only at the last moment, even permitting itself, at times, to be stroked by the hand. The eggs, too, are protectively colored and difficult to see as they lie on their bed of dry leaves. The so-called early spring "nuptial song of the Woodcock," accompanying late evening and early morning aerial flights, has always attracted the intense interest of bird students, for the exact nature of some of the notes produced is not clearly understood. The three outer wing feathers are much narrowed and stiffened and just how much this aeolian-harp-like arrangement has to do with the "song" has been a much mooted question. Both sexes have exactly the same attenuated wing feathers, and if this is really a musical instrument it suggests that both birds take part in the performance, but nearly all authors assume that it is only the male that mounts aloft and "sings" to his mate below. The setting for the act is usually a bush-grown meadow or brushy, springy upland, and the time twilight, evening, and morning. The bird at first may strut with tail raised and expanded and head drawn in, or may walk quietly about, uttering meanwhile a loud *zeeip* or a soft guttural note. Suddenly it springs into the air and flies off at a rising angle, circling higher and higher in increasing spirals until it looks like a mere speck in the sky; during the upward flight it whistles continuously, twittering musical notes, like *twitter, itter, itter, itter,* repeated without a break. These notes may or may not be caused by the whistling of the wings. Then comes the true love song—a loud, musical, three-syllable note—sounding like *chicharee, chicharee, chicharee,* uttered three times with only a slight interval between the outbursts. This song is given as the bird flutters downward, circling, zigzagging, and finally volplaning down to the ground at or near the starting point. The bird soon begins again the *zeeip* notes and the whole act is repeated again and again.

The Woodcock is largely crepuscular or nocturnal in its activities, spending the day in damp coverts, boring for food in the soft soil with its long, heavy bill. By a special anatomical arrangement the outer one-third of the upper mandible can be raised somewhat, independently of the rest of the bill, enabling the bird to seize the worm for which it is searching and tease it out of its lair without the necessity of opening the base of the bill, which is held in the firm surface soil. The eyes are placed far back and high in the head, thus enabling the bird to "look through the back of the head," as William Beebe says, and so keep watch for an enemy from above while probing in the mud.

PLATE 30

AMERICAN WOODCOCK

Scale about one-half

IN DISPLAY (AFTER FUERTES)

PLATE 31

SNIPES AND SANDPIPERS (Family *Scolopacidae*)

The COMMON or WILSON'S SNIPE, *Capella gallinago* (10.28-11.20), in the Western Hemisphere breeds in Alaska and Canada and over much of the northern United States from coast to coast chiefly northward; it winters commonly in the southern United States, West Indies, and south through Mexico and Central America to Colombia and southern Brazil, sparingly farther north.

The Common Snipe is the "Jack Snipe" or "Jack" of sportsmen. It dwells by preference in miry meadows and quaking bogs, and it requires no little exertion, combined with unruffled nerves and quick unerring action, to bag the unexpected bird as it suddenly springs from cover and darts away in zigzag, uneven course just above the waving grass. The long bill of the Snipe is used in probing for food in shallow water and ooze, rather than for boring in soft soil as is the case with the Woodcock. In the fall the Snipe frequently leaves the concealment of the grassy meadows and may be seen singly or even in considerable numbers on exposed mud flats or wading in the water along the shores of lakes and streams, industriously searching the bottom and sometimes in its eagerness submerging the whole head and neck. When flushed suddenly it utters an explosive, harsh *scaipe*.

Like the Woodcock and many other shore birds, the Common Snipe has a so-called flight song, which may be heard mornings and evenings, on moonlight nights, on still, cloudy days, or even in the full glare of sunlight. The bird, rising to a considerable height (150 feet or more) above the meadow that is its home, circles round and round on rapidly vibrating wings in an ever-widening orbit. At short intervals it darts suddenly and obliquely downward, producing at the same time a peculiar, hollow, whirring note which has been described as "bleating" or "drumming." This note is low-pitched and rather fugitive in character and is one of the eerie and weird sounds in nature, coming as it does from high in the heavens and seemingly from nowhere in particular. It takes careful searching to find the tiny, drifting object, and no little effort is required to keep it in view and to realize that it is really the source of the sound. This aerial performance of the Snipe has aroused even more interest and led to greater argument as to the exact origin of the sounds than has the similar performance of the Woodcock. It is now generally agreed that the whistling notes of the Woodcock are produced by air rushing through the narrowed, outer wing feathers, and it seems equally well established that the "drumming" of the Common Snipe, which with that species constitutes the entire "song," is caused by the air rushing past rigid, outer tail feathers. Thus, the "song" of the Woodcock is partly instrumental, while that of the Common Snipe is wholly so. Occasionally the circling bird utters a few cackling notes, such as are usually given when the bird is perched on the top of some dead tree or stub.

The dowitchers, known among sportsmen as the Gray Snipe (fall plumage), Robin Snipe, or Red-breast, range over North America and northern South America, breeding in the far north and wintering from the southern United States and the West Indies south to Ecuador. A spring flock of plump, long-billed birds with pale chestnut underparts, looking something like the Common Snipe but feeding on mud flats or flying in close rank instead of hiding singly in the grass, will prove on close examination to be dowitchers. In the fall when the underparts are gray they are easily mistaken for the Common Snipe. The dowitchers are tame and unsuspicious birds permitting a close approach as, with their long bills, they probe the shallow water or oozy mud on which they spend so much of their time. There are now two species of dowitchers recognized, the LONG-BILLED (*Limnodromus scolopaceus*) and the SHORT-BILLED (*L. griseus*). They are so similar that distinguishing them in the field is practically impossible. It therefore seems best to refer to them simply as dowitchers.

PLATE 31

BIRD PORTRAITS IN COLOR

-WJBRECKENRIDGE-

DOWITCHER

BREEDING ADULT

FALL AND WINTER ADULT AND IMMATURE

COMMON SNIPE, ADULT

Scale of foreground figures about one-half

PLATE 32

SANDPIPERS (Family *Scolopacidae*)

Not all the so-called shore birds are confined to beaches and mud flats. Some are rather more upland than water birds, and resort to the vicinity of water only occasionally. The birds in this plate are typical waders and are shown in their natural environment where they spend most of their lives and where they obtain their food by wading in the shallows and searching the surface or probing the oozy bottom.

The GREATER YELLOW-LEGS, *Totanus melanoleucus* (12.15-15), breeds in Alaska, east across Canada to Labrador and Newfoundland, and migrates to and fro between this briefly occupied summer home and its winter home in the southern United States and southward as far as Patagonia. Non-breeding birds may be found at any time of the year over a wide area between these extremes and may wander to Bermuda and even the British Isles.

The Greater Yellow-legs is a tall, trim-looking bird that towers head and shoulders above the lesser members of the wading fraternity with which it frequently keeps company. It is now a much less abundant bird than it was formerly. It was once a much prized game bird and in the days of "bay-bird shooting" on the Atlantic coast and elsewhere, and of unlimited bags, many thousands fell annually to the guns of a veritable army of shooters. Some of the shore birds are gone never to return and all show the lasting effects of those days of "sport," open market sale, and unrestricted slaughter. Both species of Yellow-legs are birds of the mud flats and shallow sloughs, going to the uplands only during the nesting season. When alighting they stand for an instant with the wings stretched upward full length, then fold them deliberately, and quietly look about for a few moments, occasionally bobbing their heads and teetering back and forth before settling down to feed. When not alarmed they may stand for some time on one leg with the other folded up and may even hop about in this fashion before disclosing that they are not really maimed. When startled or suspicious of danger they become very noisy and their loud outcries serve to warn all other creatures in the neighborhood to be on the lookout. It is probable that this habit has given them the names "Tell-tale" and "Tattler." The voices of the two Yellow-legs are similar, and it requires a practiced ear to distinguish between them. The usual resting or peaceful note is a far-carrying, double-syllabled cry that has been likened to a yodel, and may be expressed by the words *toowhee, toowhee* with a rolling quality, pleasing and musical. Another call is a mellow *wheu, wheu, wheu* or *pheu, pheu, pheu,* which comes down from the sky in the darkness of the night as the migrating birds pass over. The note of the larger bird has been described as a "clear, flute-like tremolo whistle in a descending scale."

The LESSER YELLOW-LEGS, *Totanus flavipes* (9.25-11.15), breeds in Alaska and east through northern Canada to Ungava, south to near the International Boundary; migration, occurrence, and wintering area are about the same as of the Greater; they are uncommon west of the Rocky Mountains. The Lesser Yellow-legs is a small counterpart of the Greater in appearance, voice, and habits. Today it is still one of the commonest of the migrating waders. The breeding birds remain a surprisingly short time in the north and numerous non-breeding birds are present throughout the summer far south of the nesting grounds.

The HUDSONIAN or RED-BREASTED GODWIT, *Limosa haemastica* (14-16.75), is a bird of the Americas, breeding in the far north and wintering in southern South America. Its migration route in the upper Mississippi Valley lies along the western border. The Hudsonian Godwit in migration is more a bird of the mud flats and beaches than is the Marbled Godwit, wading and probing the shallow water, often in company with other shore birds. This species is sometimes called the Black-tailed or Ring-tailed Marlin.

PLATE 32

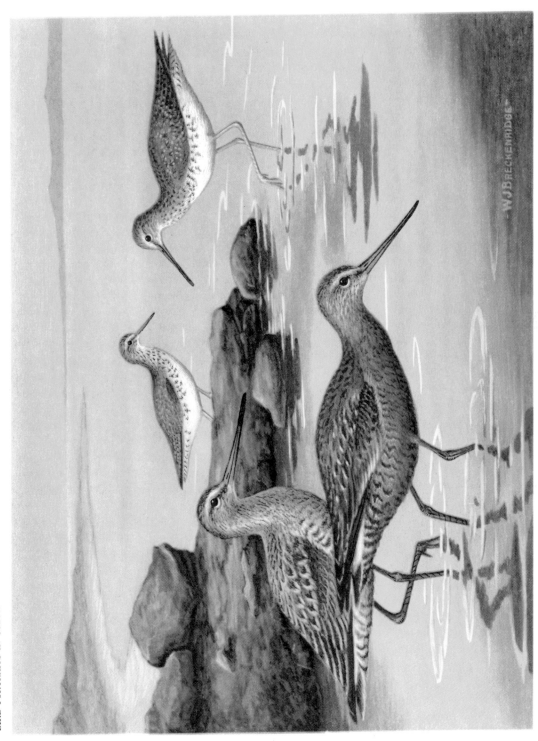

LESSER YELLOW-LEGS, ADULT

GREATER YELLOW-LEGS, ADULT

HUDSONIAN GODWIT

FALL AND WINTER ADULT AND IMMATURE

BREEDING ADULT

Scale of foreground figures about one-third

PLATE 33

SANDPIPERS (Family *Scolopacidae*)

This plate contains a group of the smaller sandpipers, one of which, the Spotted Sandpiper, is the commonest summer resident of the family in the United States and southern Canada. The others are migrants, spring and fall.

SPOTTED SANDPIPER, *Actitis macularia* (6.74-8). This familiar little bird has a vast breeding range, extending over most of North America from tree-limit in the north to the Mexican border and the Gulf states in the south. In the winter it is found from the southern part of its breeding range to southern South America, even occasionally as far as Argentina. It may wander across the seas to Greenland, Great Britain, Belgium, and Germany.

The Spotted Sandpiper or, as it is variously called, the Teeter Snipe, Teeter-tail, Peet-wit, and Tip-up, is everywhere common as a nesting bird in all suitable places throughout North America. It is not at all particular as to the character of the surroundings so long as there is a stream or open water and a suitable shore line. Mud flats are not especially fitted to its taste but it may occasionally be seen there. When startled from the water's edge it sounds a mellow *peet-weet* and darts away just above the surface on rapidly vibrating, down-curved wings, gliding a few feet now and then and describing a widespread curve to an alighting place ahead. It lays its spotted eggs in a simple nest on gravel beaches or sand bars and not infrequently in upland fields or pastures, when it may be seen poised on the top of a stake, fence post, or on the summit of a dead stub, on the lookout for possible danger. The young leave the nest as soon as they are dry from the egg and can then run about and teeter and sound the *peet-weet* call just like their parents. This little sandpiper gets the name Teeter-snipe or Tip-up from a curious habit of teetering the rear part of the body. The Solitary Sandpiper bows in proper fashion with the fore part of the body, while the Spotted bows with the hinder part! During the mating and nesting season there may be heard a pretty little flight song. Rising to no great height not far from the nest, the bird poises or moves slowly about on tremulous, stiffened wings, and with head thrown up delivers a rapid succession of not unmusical notes resembling somewhat the usual *peet-weet* utterance. The Spotted Sandpiper, both old and young, in common with other shore birds is a good swimmer and in the face of danger may dive and swim for some distance beneath the surface.

The STILT SANDPIPER, *Micropalama himantopus* (7.50-9.25), so called because of its long legs, breeds in the arctic regions of North America and winters chiefly in South America as far south as Chile and Uruguay; its main migration route is through the interior of North America, the West Indies, and Central America.

The Stilt Sandpiper is a regular but not very common migrant in the upper Mississippi Valley, occurring in greatest numbers on the western prairies. It travels in flocks, sometimes of a hundred birds or more. Shallow pools are its choice, where it can wade about freely with the water usually up to the body. It is a deep prober, often submerging the entire head and neck as it thrusts its bill vertically into the soft, oozy bottom.

The PECTORAL SANDPIPER, *Erolia melanotos* (8-9), is an American bird, breeding in the far north and wintering in South America as far south as Patagonia. It is at times a far-wanderer, having been found in Hawaii, New Zealand, Japan, and England.

The Pectoral is still one of the common migrating sandpipers. Although seen usually in flocks on mud flats and wading in shallow ponds, it has also a fondness for the insect life of short-grass meadows and upland fields, which has won for it the common name of Grass Snipe. From its creaky notes comes another common name, Creaker.

PECTORAL SANDPIPER, ADULT

STILT SANDPIPER

FALL AND WINTER ADULT   BREEDING ADULT

SPOTTED SANDPIPER

FALL AND WINTER ADULT AND
IMMATURE

BREEDING ADULT

Scale of foreground figures about one-half

PLATE 34

SANDPIPERS (Family *Scolopacidae*)

The sandpipers assembled in this illustration are among the smallest of their kind and are the most difficult to name correctly in the field, not only for the amateur but also for the more advanced student. The fact that these species are usually associated in the same flock assists somewhat in distinguishing the birds. However, at best it will require repeated and close observation to make identifications certain. The careful student of the living birds will come to recognize that each species has some little mannerism or peculiar habit that will assist more or less in placing it. Such traits, of course, can only be learned by constant and intelligent watching. It will be noticed in the illustration that the Semipalmated Sandpiper has a stouter and stubbier bill than the Least and is a trifle larger and a shade lighter in general color. Baird's is larger than either, it has a buffy suffusion about the head and neck, and the back is "scaled," because of the white feather-tips. The latter character is most marked in the fall birds.

The LEAST SANDPIPER, *Erolia minutilla* (5-6.76), breeds in Alaska and across northern Canada to Newfoundland and Nova Scotia; it winters in the southern United States and south through the West Indies and Central America to central Patagonia. Tiny as it is, it has at times crossed the seas to Europe.

The Least Sandpiper is one of the most diminutive of its kind. It is common in flocks of considerable size in both migrations, and not a few non-breeding birds remain through the summer. It is to be looked for, associated with other waders, on mud flats and sand bars. With its small relative, the Semipalmated, it usually feeds on the higher, drier parts of the flats and when not in motion it is almost invisible against the dark background of mud, while the lighter-colored Semipalmated is more plainly seen. Like most of the shore birds the Least has a flight song on its northern breeding grounds, which has been described as a short, sweet trill repeated over and over again as the bird circles around on quivering wings. The usual call-note is a musical *peep,* from which comes one of the common names, "Peep." In common with other species it is also called the "Stint."

The SEMIPALMATED SANDPIPER, *Ereunetes pusillus* (5.50-6.86), breeds from northeastern Siberia across arctic North America to northern Labrador and winters from the southern United States south through the West Indies and Central America to Patagonia. It migrates mainly east of the Rocky Mountains; it has been taken in the British Isles.

The Semipalmated is a close companion of the Least. They travel together in the same flock but in the Mississippi Valley the former usually outnumbers the latter. In addition to the characters given above it will be found on close inspection that the legs of the Semipalmated are black, instead of yellowish-green as in the Least. The partly webbed toes of this species are rarely visible in the field. It is sometimes called the Black-legged Peep and Ox-eye.

BAIRD'S SANDPIPER, *Erolia bairdii* (7-7.60), like the last two species breeds in arctic North America and winters in southern South America, migrating chiefly through the interior of North America, Central America, and northern South America. It may wander to England.

Baird's Sandpiper is a plain-colored little wader, only a trifle larger than the Peeps, and is one of the most difficult of the smaller shore birds to recognize in the field. Its buffy head, neck, and upper breast, scaled back, and a peculiar trick, when feeding, or running ahead for a few steps and then stopping abruptly with one leg in advance of the other, or one foot raised from the ground, may aid in placing it.

PLATE 34

BIRD PORTRAITS IN COLOR

SEMIPALMATED SANDPIPER
FALL AND WINTER, IMMATURE   BREEDING ADULT

BAIRD'S SANDPIPER
FALL AND WINTER, IMMATURE

BREEDING ADULT

LEAST SANDPIPER
FALL AND WINTER ADULT   BREEDING ADULT

Scale of foreground figures about one-third

PLATE 35

SANDPIPERS (Family *Scolopacidae*)

Of the four sandpipers grouped in this plate only one, the Willet, is a shore bird in the sense that it habitually haunts the margins of bodies of water and shallow sloughs. The others feed and spend most of their time on the upland, visiting shores and muddy flats only occasionally. In this respect they are like certain of the plovers.

The BUFF-BREASTED SANDPIPER, *Tryngites subruficollis* (7.50-8.90), breeds along the arctic coasts of Alaska to northern Mackenzie, and winters in Argentina and Uruguay; its main line of migration is through the interior of North America; it is rare and irregular elsewhere. It has been found as a wanderer in Bermuda, the West Indies, Europe, and Japan.

The little Buff-breasted Sandpiper is now an uncommon, even rare, bird almost everywhere. By nature and habit it is more of a plover than a sandpiper, and during migrations the aerial evolutions of the flocks are very like those of the Golden Plover, with which it is often associated. Unlike others of its kind it is largely silent. The underside of the wings is beautifully mottled and dotted with dull black on a pale background, which is effectively displayed by holding the wings aloft in the nuptial performance.

The UPLAND PLOVER, *Bartramia longicauda* (11.50-12.56), is not a plover except in its upland habits, and was formerly called the Bartramian Sandpiper or Tattler, after William Bartram, the Philadelphia botanist, for whom it was named by Alexander Wilson. Its breeding range covers most of North America except the extreme southern part, but in recent years it has disappeared from, or become scarce over, much of this area. It winters on the pampas of southern South America.

The history of the Upland Plover is a sad tale of wanton destruction that has seriously threatened a valuable and once abundant bird. The fact that it was an excellent table bird, was tame and unsuspicious, and was unprotected at the very season when it was most easily killed, combined with the extensive cultivation of the virgin prairie on which it lived, led to its disappearance. In recent years it is becoming more numerous and if let alone may reestablish itself to some extent. The wide, limitless prairies are preeminently the home of Bartram's Sandpiper. There it was once abundant and nested, and its long-drawn, melodious *quail-le-e-e-e-e-e,* a sweet, tremulous, plaintive whistle, came from far and near and was one of the most appealing and entrancing calls uttered by any plains bird.

The MARBLED GODWIT, *Limosa fedoa* (16.38-17.62), in the days of its former abundance, was one of the most conspicuous and noisy summer-resident birds of the upper Mississippi Valley prairies. Its present scarcity in that region has left a sad void to those who knew it of old. It winters in the southern United States, south to Ecuador and Peru. When met with on its nesting grounds the Marbled Godwit will be found to have a variety of loud notes, the most common and unmistakable, expressing worry or alarm, being a shrill *go-wit, go-wit, go-wit,* with strong emphasis on the last syllable, or *go-it, go-it, go-it,* with the emphasis reversed, from which comes its vernacular name.

The WILLET, *Catoptrophorus semipalmatus* (14.50-17), as a species has a breeding range covering most of North America south from southern Canada, also the Bahamas and the Greater Antilles; it winters from the southern United States to South America as far as Brazil and Peru. The eastern and western birds are separated as closely allied subspecies.

The Willet is a bird of the mud flats, beaches, marshy borders of lakes, meadows, and, less frequently, of the adjacent uplands. It has a variety of notes, one a simple *willet, willet,* and another a "long, musically whistled *pill-will-willet.*"

W.J.BRECKENRIDGE

WILLET, ADULTS

MARBLED GODWIT, ADULT   UPLAND PLOVER, ADULT

BUFF-BREASTED SANDPIPER, ADULT

Scale of foreground figures about one-fourth

PLATE 36

SANDPIPERS (Family *Scolopacidae*) AND TURNSTONES (Family *Charadriidae*)

Although all the birds in this plate are shore birds, only two are members of the sandpiper family. The third, the Ruddy Turnstone, is today placed in a subdivision of the plover family, though in its taper-pointed, unmodified bill, well-developed hind toe, transversely scaled legs, and general habits it seems to be in rather alien company.

The SOLITARY SANDPIPER, *Tringa solitaria* (7.50-9), as a species occurs in the summer months over all of Canada and the northern United States but, so far as is definitely known, breeds only north of the United States. It winters from the southern United States (casually) south as far as Argentina. It has wandered to the Galapagos Islands, Bermuda, and Great Britain. The eastern and western birds are separated as closely allied subspecies.

The Solitary Sandpiper is a common, sometimes an abundant, spring and fall migrant through the Mississippi Valley, and a few remain all summer in the northern part, but there is no positive evidence that it nests south of the Canadian boundary. It is usually found alone or in pairs along wooded streams or about forest lakes and ponds. In such places it may be seen poised on boulders and fallen tree trunks or wading in the water like the Spotted Sandpiper, which is the only other sandpiper that regularly seeks such surroundings. The Solitary, when it alights, raises its wings high above its back for a moment before folding them, and then, turning slowly about, bobs its head and bows its body in an amusingly dignified manner. When flushed it utters a few sharp, whistling notes and rises abruptly and quickly to a considerable height, unlike the Spotted, which skims off close over the water. During migration the Solitary may be found frequently on mud flats and sand bars with other waders.

The nesting habits of the Solitary Sandpiper are unique among American shore birds, the only parallel being those of the closely related Green Sandpiper of Europe. All the eggs thus far found—and they are still comparatively few in number—have been discovered in the deserted nests of robins, waxwings, grackles, jays, kingbirds, and blackbirds, which were from four to forty feet from the ground and usually near lakes or ponds.

The RUDDY TURNSTONE, *Arenaria interpres* (7.75-9.40), is a species that is practically cosmopolitan in its distribution. It nests in the circumpolar tundras and in the New World it winters in the southern United States south to Brazil and Chile.

The Ruddy Turnstone is chiefly an inhabitant of salt-water beaches, but when migrating passes through the interior in fair numbers, especially in the spring. It is tame and unsuspicious as it follows the water line, adroitly turning over stones and other small objects with a quick flip of its strong bill, from which habit is derived its common name.

The WHITE-RUMPED SANDPIPER, *Erolia fuscicollis* (6.75-8), is another little wader that makes the long journey twice each year between a breeding ground in arctic North America, west from Baffin Island, and a winter home in southern South America. It has been known to wander across the seas to distant lands—the Azores, Great Britain, and Franz Joseph Land.

The White-rump, when passing through the upper Mississippi Valley, keeps mostly to the western prairies. It associates with the other smaller sandpipers on mud flats and beaches. It is larger than the "Peeps" and resembles Baird's most closely, but the white rump will distinguish it when in full plumage.

PLATE 36

WHITE-RUMPED SANDPIPER
FALL AND WINTER ADULT
BREEDING ADULT

RUDDY TURNSTONE
BREEDING ADULT   FALL AND WINTER ADULT

SOLITARY SANDPIPER
BREEDING ADULT
FALL AND WINTER ADULT

Scale of foreground figures about one-third

PLATE 37

SANDPIPERS (Family *Scolopacidae*)

The three kinds of sandpipers grouped in this plate are all spring and fall migrants through the United States. They all breed in the far north and during migration are common on the seacoasts, but they also occur in the interior—the Dunlin in large numbers, the Sanderling in little scattered parties, and the Knot chiefly as a rather rare straggler.

The KNOT, *Calidris canutus* (10-11), as a species occurs nearly throughout the world, breeding in the far north and wintering chiefly in the far south.

There are very few records of the Knot in the Mississippi Valley. In its long migrations it follows seacoasts chiefly. Previous to the nineteenth century it was very abundant on the Atlantic coast, which is its chief migration route in North America, but its numbers were greatly reduced by excessive shooting from which the species has only partially recovered. It was variously called by hunters the Gray-back, Robin Snipe, Red-breasted Snipe, and Wahquoat. The last name is derived from one of its rather few notes, for it is said not to be a noisy bird.

The DUNLIN or RED-BACKED SANDPIPER, *Erolia alpina pacifica* (7.60-9.25), is a shore bird that breeds in the far north but does not go to the Southern Hemisphere in winter. An Old World race, *P. a. alpina* nests along the arctic coasts and reaches northern Africa and southern India in winter; the American race breeds in northeastern Siberia, Alaska, and across northern Canada to Hudson Bay, being seen in migration in the Great Lakes region, and wintering mainly in the southern United States and north on the Pacific coast to British Columbia.

The Red-backed or Black-bellied Sandpiper is well represented in both migrations in the Mississippi Valley. Among a mixed flock of small waders, seen in the spring feeding on a sand bar or mud flat, the Red-backs are apt to keep by themselves and can readily be picked out as a group of rather stocky, short-legged birds with bright rufous backs, black bellies, and long bills slightly decurved at the tip. When startled they fly with the others but the moment they alight are again side by side. In feeding they are deep probers, moving about rather deliberately, pausing now and then to step up on some exposed clod and rest awhile with head drawn in. They are always tame and unsuspicious, permitting a close approach entirely in the open. The plain-colored fall birds may be confusing, but the short legs and decurved bill will assist in placing them.

The SANDERLING, *Crocethia alba* (7-8.75), is world-wide in its distribution, breeding on arctic coasts and islands, and in the Americas wintering in the southern United States, Bermuda, and south as far as Patagonia, in the Old World south as far as southern Africa, Australia, and the islands of the South Pacific. "To the ends of the earth and back again extend the migrations of the sanderling, the cosmopolitan globe trotter; few species, if any, equal it in world-wide wanderings" (Bent).

In the Mississippi Valley the Sanderling can usually be found in the latter part of May and early June in little flocks, passing northward in company with other late migrating waders. It is less frequent in the fall. It is there a wanderer from the ocean beaches where it abounds. The Sanderling is conspicuous among the other waders because of its light appearance, especially when in fall plumage.

PLATE 37

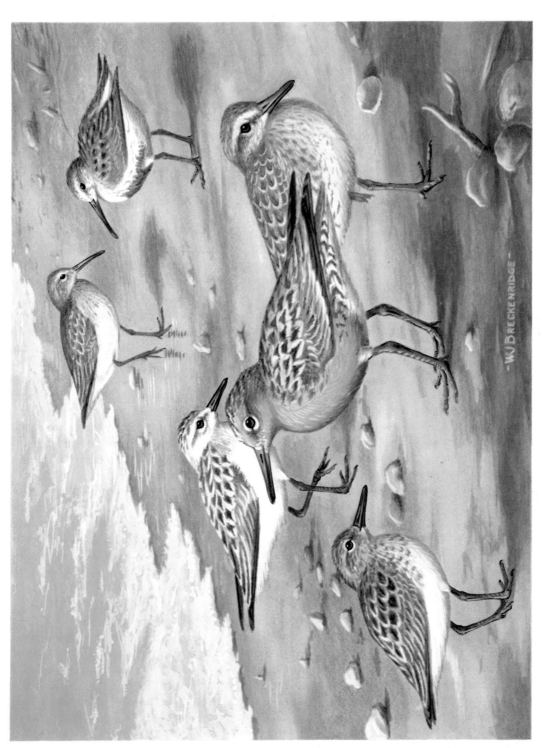

- W J BRECKENRIDGE -

SANDERLING
FALL AND WINTER ADULT

BREEDING ADULT

DUNLIN

FALL AND WINTER ADULT

BREEDING ADULT

KNOT

BREEDING ADULT

FALL AND WINTER ADULT

Scale of foreground figures about one-third

PLATE 38

PHALAROPES (Family *Phalaropodidae*)

The phalaropes are small, sandpiper-like birds, which differ conspicuously from the other members of the order in their lobed or scallop-margined toes, greatly compressed shanks, and dense and compact plumage, like that of coots and gulls. These characters are mainly adaptive and enable the phalaropes to swim with ease. In fact they are as much at home upon the surface of the water, even that of the ocean, as are any of the true swimming birds. The bill is very slender, almost needle-like. The female is larger than the male and, in breeding plumage, is much more highly colored. After laying the eggs she leaves their incubation and the care of the young to the male, but usually, if not always, she remains near by to see that he attends to his duties and to join with him in protesting against any intrusion upon their particular bit of meadow. Only three species are known, all of which occur in America; one of them is found only there, the other two in the Old World as well.

The illustration shows the two species of phalaropes that occur regularly in the interior of North America. One, the Wilson's Phalarope, is a summer-resident, breeding bird; the other, the Northern Phalarope, is a migrant, spring and fall. A third species, the Red Phalarope, largely a bird of the oceans, has been recorded as a wanderer at various places far from the seacoasts.

Wilson's Phalarope, *Steganopus tricolor* (9.50-10), belongs to the Americas only, breeding chiefly in the north central United States and neighboring Canadian provinces, and west to the Pacific coast; it winters in southern South America; and it occurs in migration on the Atlantic and Pacific coasts.

Wilson's Phalarope is one of the most beautiful and attractive of the many shore birds. The large, handsome female may receive more attention than her smaller, more plainly garbed mate, but both are charming, graceful birds and are ever a delight and joy to the bird lover. Previous to about 1900 it was an abundant summer resident throughout most of the upper Mississippi Valley, every large slough or shallow lake harboring many pairs during the nesting season. It then almost entirely disappeared for a time, but is now back again in many of its old haunts, though in much reduced numbers.

Wilson's Phalarope is more a bird of the mud flats and meadows than is the Northern, but not infrequently it may be seen wading in shallow water, probing the bottom with head and neck submerged, or engaged in a curious procedure consisting of spinning quickly round and round and deftly picking from the surface food particles stirred up from the bottom by its rapidly moving legs. A whole flock may be seen at times gyrating at once in this dizzy fashion. The voice of this phalarope is soft and mellow, and the usual note is a little *trump, trump,* uttered in a subdued, musical manner as they feed together, or in a worried, more forcible tone when circling about over the head of an intruder.

The Northern Phalarope, *Lobipes lobatus* (6.40-8), belongs to both the Old and New Worlds. It breeds in the far north and winters in southern South America, Africa, and southern Asia, and often out at sea. In North America it migrates chiefly at sea off both coasts, and in less numbers through the interior of Canada and the United States.

The Northern Phalarope is a graceful, dainty, gentle little bird, and the name "Fairy Duck," which has been applied to it, is very fitting, for its actions, as it swims lightly about, suggest nothing so much as a tiny, elfin, duck-like creature. It spins and picks its invisible food from the surface just as does the Wilson's. The white bar in the wing, conspicuous in flight, will distinguish it from Wilson's.

PLATE 38

NORTHERN PHALAROPE

FEMALE, BREEDING ADULT

MALE, BREEDING ADULT

FALL AND WINTER ADULT

WILSON'S PHALAROPE

FEMALE, BREEDING ADULT

MALE, BREEDING ADULT

IMMATURE, FALL AND WINTER

Scale of foreground figures about one-half

PLATE 39

GULLS AND TERNS (Family *Laridae*)

Gulls and terns are long-winged, web-footed, densely feathered, mostly white (adults) birds, of graceful flight and attractive appearance, and are seen most commonly over oceans and about lakes and the larger watercourses. About eighty species are distributed throughout the world; nearly half of these are of regular occurrence in North America. The family is divided into two subfamilies, the gulls (*Larinae*) and the terns (*Sterninae*). Gulls are more heavily built birds than are terns, with more or less hooked instead of pointed bills, usually even or rounded instead of forked tails, broader and less pointed wings, and are slower in flight. Gulls when flying usually carry the bill pointed forward, while terns carry it pointed downward. When feeding over water gulls commonly alight on the surface and pick up floating objects, while terns dive from a height. When feeding over land both are expert flycatchers, seizing flying insects with ease and agility. Gulls rest on the water, while terns seek resting places elsewhere. Gulls are valuable scavengers about harbors and similar places, but terns usually take living prey.

The HERRING GULL, *Larus argentatus smithsonianus* (22.50-26), is one of several races of a species that is found throughout the Northern Hemisphere, breeding chiefly in the northern part of its range. This is the gull seen commonly in spring and fall flying leisurely about the larger lakes and along the main streams and following in the wake of steamers on the Great Lakes. The name "Sea Gull" is commonly applied to this bird and its near relative the Ring-billed Gull, for to the minds of most people gulls suggest the sea.

The RING-BILLED GULL, *Larus delawarensis* (18-21), is a North American species, breeding mainly on the interior lakes of Canada and the northern United States; it winters from the southern part of its breeding range to the Gulf coast and southern Mexico. The Ring-bill is a small edition of the Herring Gull and not easily distinguished in the field except on close inspection. Many non-breeding birds remain about the large bodies of water all summer, south of the breeding area.

BONAPARTE'S GULL, *Larus philadelphia* (13-14.25), breeds in northwestern North America, and winters chiefly on the Atlantic, Pacific, and Gulf coasts as far south as southern Mexico. It has been found as a wanderer in distant lands. Unlike its near relatives this gull builds its stick nest in small evergreen trees and on stumps, often in places remote from water. Flocks of a dozen or more, composed of young birds and non-breeding adults, may spend the summer far south of the nesting range.

FRANKLIN'S GULL, *Larus pipixcan* (14-15.50), breeds in the prairie sloughs and reedy lakes of the interior of North America north from Iowa and Utah, and winters from the Gulf coast as far south as Peru, Patagonia, and Chile—the only gull that breeds in the north and migrates south of the equator. Franklin's Gull nests in vast colonies in the central prairie regions of the northern United States and in the southern provinces of Canada. In its migrations through the Mississippi Valley it leans commonly to the westward, avoiding the forested areas. It feeds so extensively on insects, especially grasshoppers, that it is a valuable asset to the farmer. It is a common sight on the western prairie to see large flocks of Franklin's Gulls following the breaking plows and alighting in the freshly turned furrows to pick up the insects and worms brought to view.

The GLAUCOUS GULL or BURGOMASTER, *Larus hyperboreus* (26-32), is a rare winter straggler from the north into the interior of the United States, but is of more frequent occurrence along the coasts. The absence of black on the ends of the wings distinguishes it from the Herring Gull.

Alan Brooks -

FRANKLIN'S GULL

BONAPARTE'S GULL

IMMATURE   BREEDING ADULT   BREEDING ADULT   IMMATURE

RING-BILLED GULL   BREEDING ADULT   HERRING GULL

IMMATURE   BREEDING ADULT

GLAUCOUS GULL   IMMATURE, FIRST FALL AND WINTER

IMMATURE, SECOND WINTER

Scale about one-seventh

PLATE 40

GULLS AND TERNS (Family *Laridae*)

Because of their long, forked tails and graceful, easy flight, terns are often called "Sea Swallows," though they are by no means confined to the seas. All four species shown in the illustration are common in the interior of North America either as migrants or as nesting birds.

The COMMON TERN, *Sterna hirundo* (13.65-15), is nearly cosmopolitan in its distribution, breeding in many countries almost throughout the Northern Hemisphere, and wintering chiefly in the Southern Hemisphere. In North America the Common Tern nests in colonies on rocky and sandy islands in the larger northern lakes and along the North Atlantic coast. It is also to be found on the islands of the South Atlantic and Gulf coasts.

FORSTER'S TERN, *Sterna forsteri* (14.50-16.25), is a bird of North America, breeding in widely scattered localities, both north and south, and wintering from the southern United States south to Guatemala. In the upper Mississippi Valley Forster's Tern breeds in small colonies in the sloughs and weedy lakes of the prairie region under very different conditions from its close relative, the Common Tern.

Forster's and the Common terns, in the black-capped spring and breeding plumage, are not easy to distinguish in the field. The immature fall birds, with the difference in the black areas on the head and the dark band on the wing of the Common, are more easily distinguished.

The CASPIAN TERN, *Hydroprogne caspia* (19-23), is found in both the Old and New Worlds. It breeds in colonies at widely separated localities, both in the north and south, and winters along the coasts of the continents. The Caspian Tern, as it wings its way over our larger lakes, is a large handsome bird, and its swift, vertical plunges into the water are spectacular performances. The big red bill is plainly evident, and the tail is rather short and not as deeply forked as in the smaller, black-capped terns.

The BLACK TERN, *Chlidonias nigra surinamensis* (9.50-10.38), is the American representative of a species that occurs in both the Old and New Worlds. The American race breeds over much of the northern United States and Canada, and winters mainly in South America; it migrates chiefly through the interior. This little tern, which, unlike others of its kind, is largely black in full plumage, is one of the most common and generally distributed water birds of the upper Mississippi Valley. Nearly every slough and marshy lake has its quota of nesting Black Terns. When feeding, it winnows its way back and forth over open water or the upland, searching for finny prey in the one instance and for flying insects in the other. At the molt in late summer a more fitting dress of white is substituted for the black, when old and young become largely white birds. Rarely an adult comes back in the spring still in the white winter plumage, and is then a conspicuous, and it may be a misleading, object among its black associates.

The LEAST TERN, *Sterna albifrons* (not in illustration), is a dainty little bird only nine inches in length; the adult is largely white with a black cap, deeply forked tail, yellow bill, and orange feet. In America it breeds chiefly from Massachusetts south along the coast to northern South America, and in the interior from Iowa and South Dakota southward; it winters from the northern Gulf coast to Patagonia. The Black Tern in the white plumage may be mistaken for the Least Tern, but the latter's small size, yellow bill, and deeply forked tail should suffice to identify it.

PLATE 40

COMMON TERN
BREEDING ADULT
IMMATURE

FORSTER'S TERN
BREEDING ADULT
IMMATURE

BLACK TERN
FALL AND WINTER ADULT (FLYING)
IMMATURE

CASPIAN TERN
BREEDING ADULT

BREEDING ADULT

IMMATURE

Scale about one-fourth

PLATE 41

PIGEONS AND DOVES (Family *Columbidae*)

Pigeons and doves are found throughout the temperate and tropical portions of the world but are most numerous in the East Indian and Australian regions. Nearly 300 species are known. Among the members of this family are some of the most beautiful birds of the world, arrayed in brilliant colors disposed in striking patterns, and some with handsome crown ornaments. In size they vary from little doves less than seven inches in length to great crowned pigeons nearly three feet long. The crests of the latter, the handsome Gouras, of the Papuan and Solomon islands, furnish the "Goura plumes" that were at one time very popular as hat ornaments.

Pigeons have bills that are swollen and soft at the base where the nostrils open, hard at the tip, and depressed in the middle—something like the bill of a true plover. The plumage is dense but easily detached from the tender skin. The young are hatched nearly naked and remain in the nest until able to fly. They are fed by both parents on a liquid substance, often called "pigeon milk," which is secreted by the enlarged crop and regurgitated into the mouth, from which the young birds suck it out by inserting the bill into the mouth of the old bird, crosswise near the base. The sexes in adult plumage are similar. Both take part in building the nest and in incubating the one or two white eggs. Pigeons and doves drink in a manner peculiar to themselves. The bill is inserted in the water up to the nostrils and the liquid is drawn up steadily without removing the bill. All other birds raise the head between sips and allow the water to run down the throat.

The PASSENGER PIGEON, *Ectopistes migratorius* (15-18), was a bird of North America east of the Rocky Mountains and north of Mexico, and wintered in the southern United States. The vast flights of the early part of the last century, as recorded by Audubon, Wilson, and others, are today almost unbelievable. It is now entirely extinct. It was destroyed by man, chiefly between 1840 and 1880, and the few remaining after the latter date soon disappeared from natural causes. They were trapped and otherwise killed at their nesting places for shipment to eastern markets by commercially organized companies. The story of the passing of the wild pigeon is a recital of man's greed and unrestrained slaughter that cannot be told here for lack of space. It can be found recounted in detail elsewhere.

The MOURNING DOVE, *Zenaidura macroura* (11-13), as a species breeds in southern Canada and south throughout most of the United States, Mexico, and outlying islands; it winters south as far as Panama.

The Mourning Dove is a seed-eater and has been favored by the cultivation of small grains. This fact together with the planting of trees on the prairies caused this species to increase greatly in numbers in recent years. The flimsy stick nest is placed at various heights in trees and not infrequently on the ground. Incubation may begin before the nest is finished, the unoccupied bird bringing additional material and passing it to the sitting bird, to be used in completing the simple structure. The Dove differs from the Passenger Pigeon, for which it is often mistaken, in its smaller size, shorter tail, more subdued colors, and by the presence, in the adult, of a black spot behind and a little below the eye, which was absent in the Pigeon. Several further differences between these birds may be noted. The Dove's wings whistle in flight; the Passenger Pigeon's did not. The Dove's note is a soft, resonant coo; the voice of the Pigeon was harsh and loud. The Dove lays two eggs; the Pigeon laid only one.

PASSENGER PIGEON
FEMALE   MALE

MOURNING DOVE
MALE

FEMALE

Scale about one-third

PLATE 42

CUCKOOS (Family *Cuculidae*) AND KINGFISHERS (Family *Alcedinidae*)

The cuckoos are a numerous and widely distributed family varying greatly in external appearance and in habits. About 125 species are recognized, but only four species are found regularly in North America. The cuckoo tribe as a whole is a curious and, in some respects, uncanny group of birds. They range in size from little, brilliantly colored birds, only five or six inches in length, to large crow- and grouse-like birds of the Old World. Many species closely resemble, in plumage, habits, and voice, other totally unrelated birds and even small mammals. There are Hawk Cuckoos, Shrike Cuckoos, Grouse Cuckoos, Pheasant Cuckoos, and Squirrel Cuckoos. More than half the species are parasitic, laying their eggs in the nests of other birds and leaving the care of the eggs and the young to the foster parents. Others build nests but lay the eggs at considerable intervals, so that the young are hatched some days apart. The more northern species are migratory but those of warmer climes are resident. Some are arboreal, others strictly terrestrial like the Road-runner of the southwestern United States. Cuckoos all have two toes in front and two behind. The young are hatched naked and there is no downy stage, the first plumage appearing early as tightly rolled pinfeathers.

The two common North American cuckoos are summer residents and are more like normal birds. They are plain-colored, slender birds of shy and elusive habit, rarely seen but often heard. They build their own nests, shabby though they be, and care for their eggs and young, often feeding them on live caterpillars. The calls of the two cuckoos are very similar—a series of *kow, kow* notes, slowing down at the finish. It requires a practiced ear to distinguish between the species. Cuckoos are valuable birds economically, as nearly half of their food is caterpillars, with many other injurious insects in addition.

The YELLOW-BILLED CUCKOO, *Coccyzus americanus* (11-12.75), is a species that breeds throughout the United States, in southern Canada, and northern Mexico, and winters in South America.

The BLACK-BILLED CUCKOO, *Coccyzus erythropthalmus* (11-12.75), breeds in southern Canada east from Alberta, and south in the United States nearly to the Gulf states; it winters in South America from Colombia to Peru.

Kingfishers are widely distributed in the world, there being nearly 100 species known. There are kingfishers that live in deserts, feeding on mice, insects, and reptiles, and nesting in holes in trees. They vary greatly in size and coloring. All have big heads, big bills, small, weak feet with the outer and middle toes united for more than half the length, and the tongue is very tiny. The young are hatched naked but are fully feathered when they leave the nest.

The BELTED KINGFISHER, *Megaceryle alcyon* (11-14.75), breeds throughout Canada and the United States, and winters mainly from the southern states south as far as northern South America, north on the Pacific coast to British Columbia. The eastern and western birds are separated as subspecies, the eastern race being the bird east of the Rocky Mountains. The loud, striking call of the Kingfisher, resembling an old-time policeman's rattle, is a common sound about our lakes and streams from the time the ice breaks in the spring until it forms again in the fall. An occasional venturesome bird remains in the north through the winter about unfrozen streams. The Kingfisher feeds chiefly on small fish, which it catches by diving for them from the air and seizing them in its big bill. The nest is a deep tunnel, excavated with the strong bill in a bank, usually near water. The young are thus raised in a dark, damp, unventilated, and foul place but seem none the worse for it.

Walter Alois Weber - 1930

YELLOW-BILLED CUCKOO   BLACK-BILLED CUCKOO
BELTED KINGFISHER
FEMALE   MALE

Scale about one-half

PLATE 43

BARN OWLS (Family *Tytonidae*) AND TYPICAL OWLS (Family *Strigidae*)

Owls are found in all climes and in nearly all countries of the world. About 135 species are known, of which about 20 species belong to North America. They may be called the nocturnal birds of prey in contrast with the diurnal birds of prey, or hawks, with which they were formerly associated, as their hooked bills, sharp talons, and predatory natures seemed to ally them with that group. But these characteristics are only adaptive, fitting them for their way of living, and not of major value in classification.

The big, round, staring eyes, directed forward as in man, are fixed in bony sockets so that the head must be turned to look sideways. This has led to a foolish belief that if one walks entirely around an owl it will twist its head off in trying to follow with its eyes, but the simple truth is that the head goes only to the halfway point and then, quick as a flash, snaps back all the way around and is ready to resume the slow, steady gaze. "Wise as an owl" is another old saying that carries no special meaning, for there are many birds wiser than owls. Owls have soft, fluffy plumage that makes little sound in flight, very sensitive ears, and eyes that see in the near-dark, which makes it possible for them to pursue successfully their nightly foragings. The female is usually larger than the male. The young are clothed with soft whitish or yellowish down. Owls lay white, nearly round eggs in open nests in trees, in holes or cavities, or in ground nests. With one or two exceptions owls are largely beneficial birds, for they feed mainly on injurious small mammals and night-flying insects. The birds they take are more than compensated for by the good they do.

The BARN or MONKEY-FACED OWL, *Tyto alba* (15-20), as a species has a wide distribution, with representatives in many parts of the world. The North American race (*T. a. pratincola*) is common throughout the more southern part of the United States, reaching the limit of its northward range in the northern states and casually in southern Canada; it is also found in Mexico and Nicaragua. It is resident and breeds throughout this range. It is an expert mouse-catcher. This comical-appearing but handsome owl is not common in the upper Mississippi Valley, but is increasing in numbers.

The LONG-EARED OWL, *Asio otus* (13-16), breeds throughout most of the wooded portions of North America, retreating in winter from the more northern parts of its range. It is a common and valuable bird as it lives largely on mice. It makes its home in tamarack swamps and other low-lying woodlands.

The SHORT-EARED or MARSH OWL, *Asio flammeus* (12.50-17), as a species is found nearly throughout the world. The North American race (*A. f. flammeus*) is resident in Canada and the United States, south to California in the west, and to New Jersey in the east; it winters from its breeding range to the Gulf coast, Cuba, and Guatemala; it also breeds in Europe and northern Asia. The Marsh Owl lives in open country, making its home on the lowlands and building its nest among the rank meadow grass. It is a beneficial bird.

The BURROWING OWL, *Speotyto cunicularia* (9-10), occurs in the Great Plains west and south from southern Canada to southern South America. It is migratory in the northern part of its range. On the western plains this little owl lives in the abandoned burrows of prairie dogs and other small animals. It has spread eastward in recent years beyond the range of the prairie dog and there lives in deserted badger dens. It raises large families, and feeds chiefly on mice, small ground squirrels, and insects, a diet which makes it a friend of the farmer. It hunts by day as well as at night. One bird usually stands as a sentinel at the entrance to the burrow, except when away foraging for the family.

BARN OWL   LONG-EARED OWL

SHORT-EARED OWL   BURROWING OWL

Scale about one-sixth

PLATE 44

TYPICAL OWLS (Family *Strigidae*)

The owls in this illustration are the big ones among the North American owls. The Snowy Owl averages heavier than the others and the female may have a wingspread of over six feet. The Great Horned Owl comes next in weight but the Great Gray appears larger, for it is clothed in a vast amount of soft, fluffy plumage and has a wingspread nearly equaling that of the Snowy. The Great Horned Owl is the only large North American owl that has conspicuous "horns" or tufts of feathers on the head. The Snowy Owl has tiny, inconspicuous "horns," nearly buried out of sight. The other owls in this group are not supplied with "horns."

The GREAT HORNED OWL, *Bubo virginianus* (20-23.75), is a bird of the Americas, occurring in one or another of its many subspecies from the arctic regions to southern South America. It is resident, breeding where found. There are several subspecies recognized, varying from a very dark form to an almost white form. The light form, generally referred to as the "Arctic Horned Owl," is an irregular winter visitor. This bird may closely resemble the Snowy Owl but is a forest rather than an open-country bird and its large "horns" are distinctive. The Great Horned Owl is the common "Hoot Owl" or "Big Cat Owl." It is a bold, fierce bird and preys to some extent upon game birds and poultry. It feeds also upon rats, mice, fish, large insects, and to a considerable extent upon rabbits. The Great Horned Owl begins nesting in late winter. It nests in an open stick nest or in a hollow tree at a considerable distance from the ground.

The SNOWY OWL, *Nyctea scandiaca* (20-27), is an inhabitant of the Northern Hemisphere and breeds on the barren grounds and islands of the far north. Many individuals wander south in the winter to milder climes. Some winters, "Snowy Owl Years," it comes south in great numbers. Most of these birds are the heavily barred young of the year, which resemble the female. The Snowy Owl lives mostly in open country where it forages, by day as well as by night, for mice, rats, and other small animals. When such food is scarce it turns to birds, including game birds and poultry.

The GREAT GRAY OWL, *Strix nebulosa* (23.50-33), as a species is circumpolar in its distribution, breeding chiefly in the far north and wandering southward in the winter. The North American race (*S. n. nebulosa*) makes its home in northern Canada and the high mountains of the western United States, and comes south in the winter rather irregularly and usually in moderate numbers. The Great Gray is a huge bird, its abundant loose plumage making it appear larger than it really is. It may be distinguished from the Barred Owl by the absence of barring on the upper breast, its greater size, and its yellow instead of black eyes. The open nest is of sticks high up in a tree.

The BARRED OWL, *Strix varia* (17-24), is a North American bird found throughout Canada and the United States. It is resident, breeding where found. There are several subspecies. The Barred Owl—also called the "Hoot Owl," for it hoots something like the Great Horned—inhabits woodlands. It also utters at times a weird, human-like scream. It is often abroad in the daytime, for like all the owls it can see very well in sunlight. It is generally believed that owls are more or less blind in the daytime but this is far from being the truth. The nest is in a hollow tree or is an open stick nest far from the ground.

GREAT GRAY OWL   BARRED OWL

GREAT HORNED OWL

SNOWY OWL   ARCTIC HORNED OWL

Scale about one-seventh

PLATE 45

TYPICAL OWLS (Family *Strigidae*)

The little SCREECH OWL, *Otus asio* (6.50-10), is found throughout the United States and Canada, and is so susceptible to the different conditions under which it lives that there are nearly a score of recognized subspecies. It is resident and breeds where found. The common bird of the northern United States and southern Canada, west to Minnesota and Manitoba, is the Eastern Screech Owl (*O. a. naevius*). This bird may be gray or red (rufous), as shown in the illustration, irrespective of age or sex. Both phases may occur in the same brood, or the parents may be differently colored. The cry of the Screech Owl is not a screech but is a series of rather soft, quavering notes uttered in a descending scale. The nest is in a hole, occasionally in a large nesting box. When feeding its young it may take many small birds but at other times lives largely on mice and large insects. On a bright moonlight night the writer has seen a whole family of Screech Owls in the tops of tall trees, darting out and catching passing insects, probably June bugs and moths, exactly like kingbirds.

The young, when they first leave the nest, usually sit close together in a tightly huddled row, awaiting the coming of their parents, and present an amusing appearance.

The HAWK OWL, *Surnia ulula* (14.50-17.50), is found in several closely related subspecies in both the Old and New Worlds. The North American race (*S. u. caparoch*) breeds in northern Alaska and Canada as far east as Labrador, and in winter appears in southern Canada and less commonly in the northern United States.

As its name implies, the Hawk Owl is in many ways more like a hawk than an owl. Its plumage is soft and its flight noiseless, like other owls, but it is almost entirely diurnal in habit, hunting its prey throughout the day regardless of whether or not the sun shines. It is usually seen perched on the top of a gaunt stub or a dead tree in a forest opening or in a tamarack and spruce swamp, watching for small mammals on the ground or for birds passing in the air. Its flight is rapid and strong, and it is quick and sure in attack. Among its notes are a screeching *ku-wee* and a whistled *ter-wita-wit, tiwita-tu-wita, wita, wita.*

The SAW-WHET or ACADIAN OWL, *Aegolius acadica* (7-8.50), is a North American species, breeding in southern Alaska, throughout Canada, in the United States as far south as Nebraska and Maryland, and in the mountains of Mexico. It is resident where found except that a few individuals may wander south of the breeding range in the United States.

This is the smallest of the owls in eastern North America. Its body is not much larger than that of a plump House Sparrow. It is a forest- and thicket-loving bird, and its diminutive size and quiet, secretive, nocturnal habits cause it to be rarely seen. The name Saw-whet comes from the fact that at times it utters notes resembling the sound produced by filing the teeth of a saw. Other notes are soft and tinkling like the sound of dropping water. Its nest is in a hole in a tree, and it lays from four to seven eggs.

The BOREAL or RICHARDSON'S OWL, *Aegolius funerea richardsoni* (8.25-12), is the American representative of a species that is found in both the Old and New Worlds. It makes its home in Alaska and northern Canada, and in winter it may wander south into the United States as far as Illinois and Pennsylvania.

The Boreal Owl seeks the seclusion of dense cover during the day and comes out to hunt in the evening. It is tame and unsuspicious and may even be taken in the hand without alarm, not because it cannot see in daylight, but because of its being unacquainted with man. The love song is a curious, liquid note, like *ting, ting, ting,* many times repeated.

BOREAL OWL   SAW-WHET OWL

HAWK OWL   SCREECH OWL

GRAY PHASE

RED PHASE

Scale about one-sixth

PLATE 46

GOATSUCKERS (Family *Caprimulgidae*) AND SWIFTS (Family *Apodidae*)

The goatsucker family is made up of about seventy species consisting of the Whip-poor-wills and Nighthawks, which are distributed nearly throughout the warmer portions of the world. They agree in having soft, owl-like plumage, wide heads, big eyes, large ear-openings, weak, more or less hooked bills, enormous mouths opening back below the eye, and small feet with the middle toe longest and the nail with a comb-like inner border. The young are covered with down when hatched. The name goatsucker came from an old superstition that these birds lived by sucking the milk from goats. The Whip-poor-wills have long, stiff bristles above the angle of the mouth, long, rounded tails, very soft plumage, and are more strictly nocturnal than Nighthawks. The Nighthawks lack the bristles at the angle of the mouth, have shorter, forked tails, and the plumage is less owl-like.

The WHIP-POOR-WILL, *Caprimulgus vociferus* (9-10.30), breeds in North America east of the Great Plains from southern Canada southward, in the southwestern United States, Mexico, and parts of Central America. The Whip-poor-will winters in the Gulf states and Mexico, south to northern South America.

The unmistakable, weird cry of the Whip-poor-will, *whip-per-rill, cluck, whip-per-rill,* is a common night sound in the upper Mississippi Valley states and adjoining parts of Canada from mid-April to nearly midsummer. The two creamy-white, blotched eggs are laid on the ground without any attempt at a nest, usually in an opening in the forest.

The COMMON NIGHTHAWK, *Chordeiles minor* (8.25-10), in one or another of its several subspecies breeds throughout North America and winters in South America, the extremes of its range being the southern Yukon in the north and Argentina in the south—the longest migration route of any North American land bird.

All through bright, sunny days the Nighthawk sits quietly, crouched low lengthways of the limb or fence rail on which it rests. As evening approaches and on dark days it rises into the upper air and circles erratically about uttering a sharp *peent, peent,* and in the breeding season swoops, every now and then, abruptly downward, the upward turn near the earth being accompanied by a loud *booming* sound. The two thickly speckled, grayish eggs are laid on the bare ground, usually in open places.

There are numerous species of Swifts found throughout the temperate and tropical parts of the world. They are mostly small birds with tiny, weak, flattened bills, the mouth opening back beneath the eye. The legs are short but the feet are rather large with much-curved, strong, and sharp claws. The "hand" part of the wing is greatly elongated, in common with the goatsuckers and hummingbirds. The flight is swift and erratic, rapid wing strokes alternating with periods of sailing. They never alight except when roosting or nesting. Their nests are curious affairs, variously placed, the materials glued together and to the support with the thick, tenacious saliva. They feed on insects captured on the wing. The only species found in the eastern United States, the Chimney Swift, belongs to a group having the tail feathers spiny-tipped.

The CHIMNEY SWIFT, *Chaetura pelagica* (4.75-5.60), breeds in the United States and southern Canada east of the Rocky Mountains. It winters south of the United States. The twittering, darting, rapidly circling little Chimney Swift is a familiar object in the sky over cities and settlements and is by no means scarce in the wilder, wooded regions, where it nests, as of old, in hollow trees.

CHIMNEY SWIFT (FLYING)   COMMON NIGHTHAWK, FEMALE (FLYING)
MALE
WHIP-POOR-WILL, MALE
Scale of foreground figures about one-half

HUMMINGBIRDS (Family *Trochilidae*)

Hummingbirds are found only in the New World. There are some 300 species, most abundant in the tropics. They vary in size from the Giant Hummer of the Andes, over eight inches in length, to the Fairy Hummer of Cuba, only two and a quarter inches long, the tiniest of birds, which builds a nest only three-quarters of an inch in width and holding eggs only a quarter of an inch in length.

Birds of this family have narrow, pointed, rigid wings operated by powerful muscles, for rapid motion and swift flight; tiny, weak feet, with rather long, curved nails, suitable for perching only; slender bills varying in length from one-fourth to five inches, usually straight but sometimes strongly curved like a sickle; an extensile, brush-tipped tongue, deeply cleft into two or more parts, each of which can be rolled into a tube for sucking nectar from flowers, which, with many small insects, forms the principal food. The nests are dainty, cup-shaped affairs usually built of plant-down and spiderwebs and covered, externally, with bits of lichen or other material, which makes them appear like a natural portion of the support on which they rest. The nest is secured in position and the materials held together by the abundant tenacious saliva of the birds. The eggs are two in number and plain white. The young are hatched naked, have short bills at first, and remain in the nest for two or three weeks.

The RUBY-THROATED HUMMINGBIRD, *Archilochus colubris* (3.25-3.85), the only species found in eastern North America, breeds in southern Canada east from Alberta, and south through the United States to the Gulf coast, west to North Dakota and central Texas; it winters along the Gulf coast and through Mexico and Central America to Panama.

This gem among the birds of eastern North America is a common summer resident and is present alike in the groves of the prairie regions and the open glades and burned-over areas in the heavy forests. It is readily recognized by its diminutive size and its habit of poising before flowers while it extracts the nectar hidden in their depths. It is sometimes confused with the hawk-moth or sphinx-moth, which has the same habit of hovering before flowers in search of food, the wings producing the same humming sound, which aids in the deception. The hummer is plain green above while the several moths are variously barred and blotched with contrasting colors.

The female Ruby-throat is an accomplished architect, for it is she who builds the marvelous and exquisite little nest, without the least assistance from her mate. The structure appears so dainty and so delicate that it seems impossible that it could weather storms and meet the requirements of an exceptionally long occupancy, but it is so securely anchored and woven about with spiderwebs and threads of saliva that it rarely fails of its purpose. Over two weeks are required to hatch the eggs and three weeks more must elapse before the young are able to leave the nest. The tiny hummers are hatched naked and for a week or ten days are very weak and puny with short, undeveloped bills. Later they grow rapidly, the bill lengthens, and, as the end of the three weeks approaches, the nest bulges and flattens, and finally they are forced out onto the rim for the last day or two. They are fed on a mixture of nectar and minute insects, which at first is squirted into their throats through the mother's tubular tongue, but later is pumped into them in a most alarmingly forceful fashion with the parent's needle-like bill thrust far down into the throat of the infant. While the male all this time is doing valiant guard duty near by he rarely if ever visits the nest, leaving to his mate all the duties of nidification from the beginning to the end. The adult male Ruby-throat is rarely seen in the northern United States after the middle of August.

RUBY-THROATED HUMMINGBIRD
MALE
FEMALE
YOUNG MALE

Scale about one-half

PLATE 47

WOODPECKERS (Family *Picidae*)

Woodpeckers are found in all parts of the world except Madagascar and the Australian region. There are some 200 species, about 20 of which occur regularly in the United States.

The typical woodpeckers form a well-marked group with characters that readily distinguish them from other birds. They have short, stout legs and nipper-like feet with two toes in front and two behind (except certain three-toed species) with which they cling to the bark of trees, supported by a stiff, pointed tail of twelve feathers used as a prop. A narrow neck and a heavy head, equipped with a strong chisel-like bill, enable them to dig out borers in hard wood and to excavate the cavities in which they nest. A remarkably extensile tongue, in most species sharp-tipped and barbed like an arrow, provides an efficient instrument for spearing larvae in their tunnels, while the sticky saliva on the worm-like body of the tongue entangles ants and other small insects with which it may come in contact. An exception is the tongue of the sapsuckers, which is but little extensile and is fringed at the end for lapping up the sap on which they feed so largely.

The North American members of this family all nest in holes that they excavate in trees (living or dead), posts, poles, etc. This is a strenuous undertaking but the work is done quickly and skillfully, both birds taking turns at short intervals. The eggs are plain glossy white and are laid on chips in the bottom of the hole without any nest. The young are hatched naked and blind, and remain in the nest longer than most of our small birds. The first plumage appears as tightly rolled quill feathers, which are rather slow in bursting, but the bird is fully feathered before leaving the nest. In their food habits woodpeckers stand very high among useful birds. Only one of our species, the Yellow-bellied Sapsucker, does any real harm.

The YELLOW-SHAFTED FLICKER, *Colaptes auratus* (12-12.75), is a North American bird and breeds from northern Alaska and Canada, east of the Rockies, south through the United States. The more northern birds retreat southward in the winter.

The Flicker has many names, among which are the Golden-winged Woodpecker, Yellow-hammer, and High-hole. It is a very common and well-known bird, nesting everywhere and migrating spring and fall in large, loosely associated companies. It feeds extensively on ants, which it collects from their holes and nests by means of a very extensile, sticky tongue, so it is very commonly seen on the ground.

The RED-HEADED WOODPECKER, *Melanerpes erythrocephalus* (9.25-9.75), is confined to North America and breeds in southern Canada from southern Saskatchewan east to southeastern Ontario and throughout most of the United States. The more northern birds are migratory.

This is a common and conspicuous bird, seen very frequently along highways, where many are killed by passing automobiles, as they make a too slow getaway. Small fruits and flying insects form a considerable part of its food. The insects are captured by hawking for them from treetops in the manner of a flycatcher. The sexes are alike in plumage.

The RED-BELLIED WOODPECKER, *Centurus carolinus* (9-10.10), is confined chiefly to the eastern half of the United States. It is resident, breeding where found.

The Red-bellied Woodpecker is a more southern species that is extending its range northward into the upper Mississippi Valley. It is a handsome bird that lives largely among the treetops. Its banded back is a good field mark in the eastern United States, but there are similarly marked birds farther west.

RED-HEADED WOODPECKER
ADULT   JUVENAL PLUMAGE

RED-BELLIED WOODPECKER
MALE   YELLOW-SHAFTED FLICKER
          FEMALE   FEMALE
                                           MALE

Scale about one-third

PLATE 48

WOODPECKERS (Family *Picidae*)

The Yellow-bellied Sapsucker, *Sphyrapicus varius varius* (7.75-8.75), is the eastern race of a species that occurs throughout most of North America, and, in winter, in the West Indies, Mexico, and Panama.

The male Sapsucker is a handsome fellow with his contrasting colors of crimson, black, and white, but he and his whole family are the evildoers among the woodpecker tribe so far as the interests of man are concerned. The Sapsucker's guilt lies in the fact that in securing the bulk of its food it does serious damage not only to forest trees but to orchards and to ornamental trees and shrubs. It lives to a very considerable extent upon the sap of trees, and to secure this it encircles the trunks with regularly placed, round holes, which pierce the cambium or sap-bearing layer of the bark and so bleed the trees of the fluid upon which their vitality depends. The oozing sap fills the holes from which the bird, at regular intervals, laps it with its brush-like tongue. As one circle of perforations becomes dry a second is drilled immediately above, then a third and fourth and so on up the trunk and out onto the larger limbs as long as the tree continues to yield a supply. A preference is shown for sugar maples, soft maples, and poplars, but no trees are exempt, conifers as well as deciduous trees being made to pay tribute. The effects upon the trees are that they are weakened, often killed. Even those surviving are scarred and disfigured for life both without and within, for the deeper borings check and discolor the wood beneath the bark, damaging it if the tree is cut and sawed for lumber.

The Sapsucker eats also many injurious insects, but the injury inflicted on trees outweighs any benefits conferred. The ordinary call is a drawling, "mewing" sound, which has given to it the name of "Squealer."

The Hairy Woodpecker, *Dendrocopos villosus* (7.25-10.25), as a species occurs over all of North America and south through Mexico to Central America. There are many subspecies in this area, differing chiefly in size and relative amounts of black and white. It is a permanent resident where found, except for the wandering southward of a few individuals of the northern populations.

The presence of the Hairy and Downy woodpeckers is probably most frequently made known by the sharp tapping sounds produced by the vigorous cutting blows of the bill as they make their way into the buried tunnels of tree-boring insects. This is especially true in the stillness of winter when these strokes echo through the frosty air with exaggerated clearness.

All birds have tongues adapted to their special food-habits, but the Hairy Woodpecker certainly has one of the most remarkable of them all. Spear-pointed, barbed, and with the posterior horns coiled around the right eye, its far-reaching thrust is most effective in extracting the hidden borers.

The Downy Woodpecker, *Dendrocopos pubescens* (5.35-6.65), as a species occurs as a permanent resident throughout North America north of Mexico.

The little Downy is an almost perfect diminutive counterpart of the Hairy. The black barring on the outer tail feathers is about the only plumage distinction. It is less a bird of the heavy timber than is the Hairy and is more frequently seen about orchards and woodlots and in the city streets and parks.

All three of these woodpeckers nest in holes in trees and lay white eggs. They will occasionally accept man-made houses.

YELLOW-BELLIED SAPSUCKER

FEMALE   MALE   JUVENAL PLUMAGE

DOWNY WOODPECKER   HAIRY WOODPECKER
MALE   MALE
FEMALE   FEMALE

Scale about one-third

PLATE 49

WOODPECKERS (Family *Picidae*)

Two of the woodpeckers shown in this illustration belong to a small group, the members of which have only three toes instead of the usual four. They are known as the Three-toed Woodpeckers and are at home in the northern evergreen forests. The males have a yellow patch on the head instead of red as in the other species.

The BLACK-BACKED ARCTIC or THREE-TOED WOODPECKER, *Picoïdes arcticus* (9.50-10), makes its permanent home in the coniferous forests of northern North America, but individuals may occasionally wander south in the winter to the middle United States. In the upper Mississippi Valley it is confined, in the breeding season, to the pine and spruce woods of northern Minnesota and Wisconsin. It excavates its nesting hole in either a dead or a live tree, usually a live one, and has the singular habit of removing the outer layer of bark for some distance around the opening, thus making the nest tree a conspicuous object in the somber forest. Both this and the next species commonly seek their food by peeling off the bark from trees and limbs, rather than by drilling for it. The Black-back is a noisy bird, uttering its shrill cries at frequent intervals and pausing now and then while at work to pound out a loud tattoo.

The NORTHERN or AMERICAN THREE-TOED WOODPECKER, *Picoïdes tridactylus bacatus* (8.60-9), is the eastern North American race of a species that occurs as a permanent resident in the northern evergreen forests and higher mountains of both the Old and the New Worlds. Individuals may wander south in the winter to more temperate climes.

This Woodpecker is a much rarer bird than the Black-back. Its habits are similar but it is much less noisy. Its smaller size and the transverse white bands on the back distinguish it from the Black-back.

The PILEATED WOODPECKER, *Dryocopus pileatus* (16-19), as a species is found throughout most of the wooded portions of North America south to central California and the Gulf states. It is resident throughout its range.

The Pileated Woodpecker, with a single exception, is the giant among North American woodpeckers, the exception being the now nearly extinct Ivory-bill of the southern states. It weighs ten ounces or over, while the little Downy barely reaches one ounce. It is a magnificent bird, nearly the size of a crow and nearly as black, but adorned with a flaming scarlet crest and showing, in flight, great white patches in the wings. The typical woodpecker flight is a succession of deep undulations, but the Pileated progresses on an almost level course, rather slowly, with occasional periods of sailing. Like the Flicker, the Pileated feeds largely on ants, an aggregate of 6680 having been counted in three stomachs. These are largely carpenter ants, which enter, from the roots, trees with decayed hearts. The great square holes, cut through the live wood near the ground in forest trees, are the work of this bird in its effort to reach the ants in the interior. Many grubs and borers are also eaten, the tongue being equipped with both a barbed and spear-like tip and a sticky body. The great nesting holes that it sometimes excavates in telegraph and telephone poles have brought it into disfavor at times, but it is too valuable a bird to be sacrificed unless under exceptional conditions. Logcock is a frequent common name for this species, and this fact, strange to say, has led to its being confused with the Woodcock. Some persons have been known to kill and eat this bird as a result of this confusion.

BLACK-BACKED THREE-TOED WOODPECKER
FEMALE

MALE

PILEATED WOODPECKER
FEMALE   NORTHERN THREE-TOED WOODPECKER

MALE   MALE   FEMALE

Scale of foreground figures about one-third; Pileated Woodpecker about one-fifth

PLATE 50

TYRANT FLYCATCHERS (Family *Tyrannidae*)

All the birds shown in the remaining illustrations, nearly half of the entire number, belong to a single order, the perching birds (*Passeriformes*), which contains more than one-half of all existing birds. These are at the top of the avian scale, anatomically and physiologically, having the highest body temperature (112°-114° Fahr.) and the most rapid heart action (400-600 beats a minute), and they live the most intense and probably the shortest lives. They agree in having a perfect perching foot, three toes in front, and one behind. This rear toe is long and on a level with the others. The young are hatched blind and naked but soon develop sparse down, which gives place quickly, in the nest, to the juvenal plumage. The young are cared for in the nest until they can fly (*altricial,* meaning to be nursed, as distinguished from *precocial*, when the young leave the nest as soon as hatched, like little chickens and ducks).

The tyrant flycatchers are found only in the New World and form a very large group, most abundant in warm countries. They have flat bills, broad at the base and provided with bristles at the angle of the wide mouth. The sexes are usually alike in color. About 95 per cent of their food consists of insects captured on the wing, and as a group they are highly beneficial birds.

The EASTERN KINGBIRD, *Tyrannus tyrannus* (8.40-9), breeds west to Washington and New Mexico and from southern Canada to the Gulf; it winters in South America.

The Kingbird is a noisy and conspicuous fellow, and from May until late summer is everywhere in forests, in orchards, on the prairies, and in the outskirts of settlements, and is one of the most frequent post-and-wire birds of the roadside. Its habit of hawking for insects from an elevated perch, and its shrill, screaming note, force it on the attention of the passer-by.

The WESTERN or ARKANSAS KINGBIRD, *Tyrannus verticalis* (8-9.50), belongs in western North America but has spread eastward in recent years and is now common as far as the Mississippi River and casual farther east; it winters in Central America. Although similar in general habits to the Eastern Kingbird, the Western is easily distinguished. The light gray back and black white-bordered tail are distinctive. The notes, too, are different —softer, more guttural, and more varied than those of the Eastern. The male has a short song of a few notes, bubbling and somewhat musical.

The OLIVE-SIDED FLYCATCHER, *Nuttallornis borealis* (7.10-8), breeds in the evergreen forests of North America, and migrates through Central America to winter in South America.

The Olive-side is a lover of high places. In the north woods it usually places its nest far from the ground in a tall pine tree, and its favorite hunting stand is the very tip of the topmost spire of a lofty spruce or tamarack. It is a noisy bird on the nesting grounds, uttering at short intervals a loud, harsh, screaming cry, broken into two parts and preceded by a short, clear, whistled note, heard only at a short distance.

The GREAT CRESTED FLYCATCHER, *Myiarchus crinitus* (8-9), as a species breeds in eastern North America from southern Canada south to the South Atlantic and Gulf states; in winter, it is found from Mexico to Colombia. It is an inhabitant of woodlands, and wherever such exist throughout its breeding range its loud, whistled *wheep, wheep,* or alarmed, far-reaching *wheek, wheek,* is to be heard from May until mid-August. Unlike the other flycatchers shown in the plate, it nests in a hole in a tree or rotten stub and occasionally in a nesting box, laying curiously streaked and spotted eggs.

George Miksch Sutton

OLIVE-SIDED FLYCATCHER   EASTERN KINGBIRD
GREAT CRESTED FLYCATCHER   WESTERN KINGBIRD

Scale about one-half

PLATE 51

TYRANT FLYCATCHERS (Family *Tyrannidae*)

The smaller flycatchers, shown in this illustration, are very difficult to recognize by appearance alone and sometimes cannot be distinguished with certainty. In the field the notes, habitats, and nests and eggs are reliable guides. The Wood Pewee dwells by preference in the forests of the uplands; the Alder Flycatcher loves the alder and willow thickets of the lowlands; the Yellow-belly chooses the wooded sphagnum bogs of the north; while the Least Flycatcher not only keeps company with all but goes farther afield and may be at home and contented in the hazel and wolfberry copses and plum thickets of open places where the others are rarely found.

The TRAILL'S or ALDER FLYCATCHER, *Empidonax trailli trailli* (5.20-5), is the eastern race of a species that breeds throughout most of North America, and winters in Central and South America as far south as Argentina. The Alder Flycatcher lives and builds its loose, rather straggly nest of grasses among the alders and willows of the lowlands. The eggs are creamy white, sparsely speckled about the larger end with reddish-brown. The notes are rather harsh and reedy, somewhat like those of the Phoebe, but with the accent on the last syllable.

The YELLOW-BELLIED FLYCATCHER, *Empidonax flaviventris* (5.10-5.80), breeds in the evergreen forests of northern North America, and winters from southern Mexico to Panama. It sinks its nest of mosses, fine rootlets, and grasses in the sphagnum beds of the wooded lowlands. The eggs are creamy white, specked at the larger end with brown. The call note, *ti-peé-a,* resembles that of the Wood Pewee but is distinctive. An "absurd little song, like the syllables *pe-wick*, is uttered almost as a monosyllable" (Hoffman).

The WOOD PEWEE, *Contopus virens* (6-6.75), breeds in eastern North America from southern Canada west to Manitoba and south to the Gulf states; it winters in Central America and in South America to Peru.

The Wood Pewee is a pleasing vocalist and its dreamy, long-drawn *pe-e-e a we-e-e* is continued through the hot days of late summer when most other birds are silent. A more pretentious effort, which may be called a song, welcomes the dawn of late spring and early summer days. Not infrequently the usual call may be heard all through the hours of night. The nest is a flat, shallow affair saddled on a horizontal limb, and is beautifully adorned with bits of lichen glued with saliva onto the outside and rim. The creamy white, brown-spotted eggs are three or four in number.

The PHOEBE, *Sayornis phoebe* (6.25-7.25), breeds in most of North America east of the Rocky Mountains, and winters in the southern United States and Mexico.

The Phoebe, or House Pewee, is the best known member of this group, as it nests familiarly about buildings, bridges, and cabins. In the wild it places its nest about cliffs. The nest is a substantial affair of moss, mud pellets, and fine grasses; the eggs are plain white. The usual note is an emphatic *phoe-be, phoe-be,* with the accent on the first syllable.

The LEAST FLYCATCHER or CHEBEC, *Empidonax minimus* (5-5.75), breeds in North America east of the Rocky Mountains, and winters from northeastern Mexico to Panama.

The Chebec is a common and widely distributed little bird. The nest is a compact, cup-shaped structure in the fork of a sapling or saddled on a limb among upright twigs. The eggs are plain white. The call is an emphatic *che-beć, che-beć.*

WOOD PEWEE   TRAILL'S FLYCATCHER
                    PHOEBE   YELLOW-BELLIED FLYCATCHER
LEAST FLYCATCHER

Scale about one-half

PLATE 52

SWALLOWS (Family *Hirundinidae*)

Swallows are easily recognized by their long wings and graceful, rapid flight. They have more or less forked tails; small, weak feet; and short, broadly triangular bills that open wide. They are tireless fliers and feed almost entirely on the wing. Their food consists chiefly of insects, including many injurious species. At migrating time they assemble in vast mixed flocks and travel chiefly by day, feeding as they go. The twittering notes of these birds are well known, but some, such as the Martin, Tree, and Barn swallows, have liquid, musical songs, which are sweet and pleasing to the ear. Swallows bathe and drink while on the wing, pausing for an instant and daintily dipping into the surface of lake or pond. There are about seventy-five species, distributed throughout the world. They are most numerous in warm countries.

The TREE SWALLOW, *Iridoprocne bicolor* (5.25-6.25), breeds over most of North America, and winters from the extreme southern United States to Cuba and Honduras.

The Tree Swallow is the first of its family to appear in the spring, a joyous creature in metallic blue and spotless white, sweeping through the air in a perfect ecstasy of flight. The natural nesting sites of the Tree Swallow are hollow stumps, cavities in rotting limbs, holes in fence posts, or old woodpecker holes if these are situated to suit its taste. Always there must be water not far away where it can feed and bathe, wheeling above it in wide circles in pursuit of insects and dipping lightly to the surface now and then with a splash of glittering wings. This swallow is as much a creature of the air as the hummingbird, yet it is a bird neighbor in the truest sense, for it will nest in a Bluebird box close to the house, raising two broods, while accepting friendly advances with no sign of resentment or alarm. The Tree Swallow may not be a true singer, but nothing could be sweeter than the soft, warbling twitter of the male as he sits near the nest—a conversational song, full of expression, so charming and irresistible that every few moments the female's bright head appears at the nest hole with an answering note. The nest is of grass, usually with an admixture of feathers. The eggs are plain white. [Contributed by MARIE ANDREWS COMMONS.]

The BANK SWALLOW, *Riparia riparia* (4.75-6.12), as a species occurs in both the Old and New Worlds. The American race (*R. r. riparia*) breeds over most of North America, and winters in South America to Brazil and Peru.

The Bank Swallow nests in colonies, excavating, with its feet, tunnels two or three feet long in the face of sand banks, and placing the nest of grasses at the inner end. The eggs are plain white. The site of a large colony of Bank Swallows is a lively and interesting study. When the young are nearly grown they sit in the entrances to the tunnels, twittering a constant appeal to their animated and busy parents, which are flying nervously backward and forward from dawn until dark bringing tiny insects gleaned from the air.

The ROUGH-WINGED SWALLOW, *Stelgidopteryx ruficollis* (5-5.75), as a species breeds over much of North America south from southern Canada, in Mexico and Central America. The resident birds in Mexico and Central America are separated as subspecies. The North American birds winter in the extreme southern United States, Mexico, and Central America.

A pair of Rough-wings usually selects a nesting place apart from other swallows, making use of a kingfisher or other hole in a bank, a crevice in a pier or rocky cliff, a drainpipe, or a similar cavity. It rarely if ever excavates its own nesting tunnel. The eggs are plain white. The name comes from the roughened outer edge of the first wing feather. The grayish-brown throat and breast distinguish it from the Bank Swallow, which it otherwise closely resembles.

BANK SWALLOW

ROUGH-WINGED SWALLOW

TREE SWALLOW

ADULT   JUVENAL PLUMAGE

Scale about one-half

PLATE 53

SWALLOWS (Family *Hirundinidae*)

The PURPLE MARTIN, *Progne subis* (7.50-8.60), breeds from the southern provinces of Canada south through the United States to central Mexico; it winters in Brazil.

The Purple Martin, the largest of our swallows, is so closely associated in our minds with dooryards and gardens that a Martin colony has come to be symbolic of community interest and simple home life. Since the early days, when the Indians in the south attracted it by tying hollow gourds to the poles of their tepees, the Martin has seemed to prefer to nest near the habitations of man rather than in crevices of rock and in hollow tree stumps as its habit formerly was and still is in the wilder parts of the country and in sparsely settled districts. The glossy white, unmarked eggs are laid in a bulky nest composed of a conglomerate of leaves, grasses, weed stems, rags, and feathers. With the advent of the young, both parents are kept busy coming and going, constantly bringing mosquitoes, squash-beetles, locusts, and flying insects of various kinds. These are taken on the wing in graceful, easy flight, not so swift as that of the Barn Swallow nor so circuitous as the sweeping flight of the Tree Swallow. In the north but one brood in a season is the rule, while farther south two, or even three, may be raised. For several weeks the Martin-house is a clamorous abode, for the young remain with the parents until late in August, after which loose flocks of considerable size may be seen circling over lakes and marshes, awaiting the time of final departure. The song is a chirruping carol, both sweet and musical, which has been likened to soft laughter. [Contributed by MARIE ANDREWS COMMONS.]

The CLIFF or EAVE SWALLOW, *Petrochelidon pyrrhonota* (5-6), breeds over most of Canada and the United States, and in Mexico; it winters, probably, in Brazil and Argentina.

Seventy-five years ago this pretty little swallow was an abundant bird throughout the Mississippi Valley, nesting in colonies under the eaves of buildings on the prairies as well as in the wooded portions. It is still present there, though in much reduced numbers so that the colonies are now objects of special interest to bird students. The explanation of the near-disappearance of this swallow is at least twofold: first, the general destruction of its nests by the farmers because of the defacement of the barns, and, second, the occupation of its nests by the House Sparrow. Farther west the Cliff Swallow is still an abundant bird, nesting in large colonies on the walls of deep canyons and rocky escarpments.

In very early times this swallow built its nest against the face of rocky cliffs, as is its habit now in the absence of white man's buildings. The nest is a remarkable structure when perfectly formed—retort-shaped, built of pellets of mud without reinforcing material, and fastened to the face of a rocky wall or under the eaves of a building. The eggs are white, spotted with brown.

The BARN SWALLOW, *Hirundo rustica* (6-7.50), as a species occurs around the world in the Northern Hemisphere. In North America it nests south to Mexico and winters in Mexico and South America.

The Barn Swallow nowadays is a bird of the farming country. Its good habits, beautiful plumage, and familiar and confiding ways have made it one of the best known and most-loved birds of the rural districts. Originally it nested in caves and on rocky faces of cliffs, but since the coming of man it has largely abandoned these primitive sites and seeks the shelter of buildings and bridges. Here, on the walls and rafters, it plasters its nest, which is made of pellets of mud reinforced with bits of straw and lined with grasses and feathers; the eggs are white, speckled and spotted with brown. The song is a series of sweet, liquid notes.

BARN SWALLOW   CLIFF SWALLOW

MALE   ADULT

FEMALE   JUVENAL PLUMAGE

PURPLE MARTIN

FEMALE   MALE

Scale about one-half

PLATE 54

JAYS (Family *Corvidae*)

This family includes the jays, magpies, ravens, and crows, and the Old World choughs. There are some hundred species, found in all parts of the world except New Zealand and parts of Polynesia. They are medium- to large-sized birds, the raven being the largest. They agree in having stout, conical bills, not notched or angled at the base, and the nostrils covered with dense tufts of feathers. The members of the crow group walk, like Blackbirds, while the jays hop. Most species are resident where found, but in northern latitudes a partial winter migration may occur. The sexes are alike or nearly so. All the birds of this group are possessed of exceptional intelligence and are quite capable of protecting themselves from their enemies by the exercise of their wits, which may explain the fact that they are not protectively colored. As pets they develop marked individual traits and are full of pranks and mischief. The ordinary notes are loud, harsh screams, caws, and croaks, but many if not all species have subdued "whisper songs," which are not devoid of musical quality. Some species can be taught to articulate words, to whistle, and to mimic sounds and laughter very accurately.

Practically all are omnivorous in their feeding habits, eating anything digestible, animal and vegetable alike, fresh or decayed as the case may be. Large numbers of injurious insects are eaten, and where these birds exist in only normal numbers the good they do probably more than offsets any harm.

The GRAY JAY or CANADA JAY, *Perisoreus canadensis* (10.70-12.10), occurs in the coniferous forests of northern North America, south in the western mountains to Arizona. It rarely wanders south of its home surroundings.

The Gray Jay is known by a variety of common names, among which are Moose Bird, Carrion Bird, Meat Hawk, Camp Robber, Whisky John, and Whisky Jack—the first four for certain of its habits, and the last two rough corruptions of the Chippewa Indian name. To make its acquaintance it is necessary to visit the north woods. There in the winter time it will be found a tame, familiar bird, coming about camps and dwellings in search of food; but at other times it seeks the seclusion of dense spruce swamps where it nests in late winter and early spring, often before the snow is gone. The nest is a bulky, substantial affair, deep inside and warmly lined with hair and feathers to protect the greenish-gray, heavily spotted eggs. It has a great variety of calls and notes, and it has been said that if one hears a strange call in the north woods it is safe to attribute it to this bird.

The BLUE JAY, *Cyanocitta cristata* (11-12.50), breeds in southern Canada east of central Alberta, in Newfoundland, and south through the United States, east of the Rocky Mountains, to the Gulf states. It is a permanent resident, breeding where found, but a limited southward movement in winter may take place.

The Blue Jay, like the crow, is a more common bird in settled regions than in the wilds. It is no doubt easier to get a living under such conditions, for it is fond of corn, small grains, fruits, and the kitchen leavings to be picked up about farm dwellings and in city yards. The jay, beautiful as it is, has fallen into disfavor because it has an unfortunate liking for the eggs and callow young of its neighbors; but this is by no means a general habit and it would seem best to overlook this fault in a bird that has so many other attributes to recommend it. It is present all through the long, cold winter, when it is about the only bright living thing in the dreary landscape. The nest, built of sticks and well lined with rootlets, is in trees, and the eggs are greenish or dull olive, thickly speckled with shades of brown.

GRAY JAY
JUVENAL PLUMAGE
ADULT

BLUE JAY
ADULT
JUVENAL PLUMAGE

Scale about one-half

PLATE 55

RAVENS, CROWS, AND MAGPIES (Family *Corvidae*)

The COMMON RAVEN, *Corvus corax* (24-27), in several subspecies is found in Europe, northern and central Asia, and North America. In North America it now breeds chiefly in the mountains of the United States and in Canada, coming south into the northern states in winter.

The Raven was once a common bird in regions where it is now rarely seen. Its present scarcity may be explained, in part at least, by the fact that many were killed by traps set for fur-bearing animals or by eating poisoned wolf-bait. The greater size, the rounded instead of square tail, pointed feathers on the neck and breast, and the croaking instead of cawing notes, distinguish the Raven from the Crow.

The COMMON CROW, *Corvus brachyrhynchos* (17-21), as a species is distributed over all of North America except the arctic regions, retreating from the northern part of its range in winter. It breeds throughout its range. It is the Eastern Crow (*C. b. brachyrhynchos*) that occurs in the upper Mississippi Valley.

Everyone knows the Common Crow, either by its coal-black dress or by its familiar cawing notes. Likewise nearly everyone has heard what a shrewd, calculating, wary creature it is, outwitting for ages past man's efforts to destroy it. Instead of diminishing in numbers it has thrived and multiplied as man has thrived and multiplied, and in the same places. In its present abundance the Crow can be regarded as an injurious and obnoxious bird, taking a serious toll from the eggs and young of both game and non-game birds, and depleting the crops of the farmer by its fondness for corn and other grains. Crow hunting by individuals as a sport may have considerable effect in reducing a local population but this often results in the incidental destruction of many valuable birds of other species. In its former normal numbers the Crow would be a valuable bird, as it destroys great quantities of injurious insects and is an excellent scavenger. Young Crows, taken from the nest, are easily tamed and make amusing though at times rather troublesome and mischievous pets. They are clever mimics of sounds and may even be taught to utter words and short phrases very plainly. The popular idea that the tongue must be split before they can talk is a myth. Young Crows have an insatiable appetite and require at least half their weight in food daily to thrive. The large, compact, stick nest is well lined with strips of bark and rootlets, and holds from four to seven greenish- or bluish-white eggs, spotted and blotched with shades of brown.

The BLACK-BILLED or AMERICAN MAGPIE, *Pica pica* (17.50-22), is the American representative of a species that is found in both the Old and New Worlds. The North American race breeds in western Canada east as far as Manitoba, and in the western United States east as far as western Minnesota and Kansas. It is a permanent resident where found, except that individuals wander in winter far east of the normal range.

The Magpie is a not uncommon winter straggler from the west as far as the upper Mississippi Valley region. It is attracted by dead animals, upon which it feeds, and may remain for some time in the vicinity of such a food supply. When on the ground it walks in the manner of the crows, but if hurried hops like the jays.

CLARK'S NUTCRACKER or CLARK'S CROW, *Nucifraga columbiana* (12-13), is a bird of western North America, and strays eastward and southward, occasionally, in the fall or winter. It is a tame bird and does not hesitate to enter settlements in search of its varied food. It may even join the chickens in the yard and take a liberal portion of their daily rations.

BLACK-BILLED MAGPIE

COMMON CROW

CLARK'S NUTCRACKER

COMMON RAVEN

Scale about one-fourth

PLATE 56

TITMICE (Family *Paridae*), NUTHATCHES (Family *Sittidae*), AND CREEPERS (Family *Certhiidae*)

The birds grouped in this illustration belong to the above three families. There are many species of titmice, widely distributed, most numerous in the Old World. They are usually small birds with soft, fluffy plumage. The American species nest in holes in trees and lay numerous white, speckled eggs. The nuthatches are a rather small group, most numerous in the Old World. They have rather stout, tapering, sharp-pointed bills and strong feet. They nest in holes and lay numerous white, spotted eggs. The creepers are a small group, of which only a single species occurs in North America. They have slender, curved, sharp-pointed bills; stiff, pointed tail feathers; and long, much-curved, sharp claws. Like the nuthatches they live on the trunks of trees, searching for their food with their tiny pick-like bills in the crevices of the bark. They place their nests beneath a loosened piece of bark and they lay numerous white, speckled eggs.

The TUFTED TITMOUSE, *Parus bicolor* (5.60-6.50), is at home in the eastern United States, south from New Jersey and Nebraska, but is extending its range northward. The Tufted Titmouse utters a *de-de-de* something like the chickadee's notes, and also has a loud, whistled *peto, peto, peto.*

The BLACK-CAPPED CHICKADEE, *Parus atricapillus* (4.75-5.75), is found in forested regions and woods along streams from Alaska to Newfoundland and from New Mexico to Virginia. It is a permanent resident where found, although occasional extensive movements do occur. Almost everyone who sees birds at all knows and loves the little chickadee. Its confiding ways and cheery *chicka-de-de-de,* winter and summer alike, endear it to all.

The BOREAL or HUDSONIAN CHICKADEE, *Parus hudsonicus* (4.80-5.25), is a species found in the evergreen forests of northern North America, wandering southward in winter. It associates commonly with its near relative, the Black-capped Chickadee. The notes are similar but the *de-de-de* is replaced by *ze-ze-ze.*

The WHITE-BREASTED NUTHATCH, *Sitta carolinensis* (5-6.15), ranges over all of southern Canada, the United States, and south to Mexico; it is a permanent resident where found. All the year around the White-breasted Nuthatch is searching the trunks and branches of city and forest trees alike for hidden larvae and insect eggs, moving upward, downward, or sideways with equal ease and agility. Its mellow *trump, trump* is a familiar sound both winter and summer.

The RED-BREASTED NUTHATCH, *Sitta canadensis* (4.10-4.75), is found throughout North America, breeding in the northern evergreen forests and south in the higher mountains. There is a partial migration of the northern birds southward in the winter as far as southern California and the Gulf coast. The Red-breast lives mostly among the branches of trees instead of on the trunks and in many ways resembles a chickadee more than a nuthatch. Its notes are weaker, more nasal, and higher-pitched than those of the White-breasted, and are uttered more rapidly.

The BROWN CREEPER, *Certhia familiaris* (5-5.75), is a species that is found throughout the greater part of the Northern Hemisphere. It winters mainly in the southern United States, but many remain throughout the breeding range. The Brown Creeper is the slender, inconspicuous, dull-colored little bird that goes spirally up the trunks of trees in a manner quite different from our other tree-trunk gleaners. It utters sharp, delicate little *screeping* notes and occasionally, in the nesting season, a low pleasing song, audible only at a short distance.

TUFTED TITMOUSE   RED-BREASTED NUTHATCH
                                          MALE
BLACK-CAPPED CHICKADEE   FEMALE

BOREAL CHICKADEE

WHITE-BREASTED NUTHATCH
                  MALE
      FEMALE   BROWN CREEPER

Scale about one-half

PLATE 57

WRENS (Family *Troglodytidae*)

The wrens of the world number about sixty-five species, of which only one belongs to the Old World. They are most numerous in the American tropics. They are small- to medium-sized birds with relatively long, down-curved bills, and dull colors. The sexes are alike and the young resemble the adults. Most species nest in cavities, but some build exposed, globular nests with a side entrance. All have querulous, scolding notes, and some are pleasing songsters.

The WINTER WREN, *Troglodytes troglodytes* (4-4.50), is a species that is found throughout North America north of the Mexican boundary, breeding in the evergreen forests of the north and on mountains; it winters south from near the southern border of its breeding range. In its summer home among the pines the marvelous song of this mite of a bird is one of the choicest bits of bird melody. During its migrations it skulks in the tangled underbrush and utters a loud sparrow-like *churp*.

The HOUSE WREN, *Troglodytes aedon* (4.50-5), is found from southern Canada south through the United States to southern Mexico; it breeds from the Mexican boundary northward. Everyone knows the House Wren, the bustling, fussy, chattering, little brown bird that explores all nooks and crannies and comes back each year to build its nest in or near the identical box that it knows as home. It is equally at home in wild places, especially the desolate burned-overs, where it nests in holes and crannies in dead stubs.

The CAROLINA WREN, *Thryothorus ludovicianus* (5.10-6), is a species that breeds in eastern United States from southern Minnesota and southern New England south to the Gulf states and northeastern Mexico. It is resident throughout this range. It is spreading northward. The song of the Carolina Wren is loud, liquid, forcible, and carries far—quite unlike that of the House Wren. The bird may be recognized by its large size, bright rufous upperparts, and a conspicuous light line over the eye.

BEWICK'S WREN, *Thryomanes bewickii* (5-5.50), breeds in the southern half of the eastern United States, north to British Columbia on the Pacific coast, and south into Mexico; it winters throughout most of its range. Bewick's Wren is similar in habits to the House Wren but it may be distinguished by the more pronounced light line over the eye; darker, less-barred plumage; and the presence of distinct white markings on the outer tail feathers. The song is also different—louder, stronger, and more far-carrying.

The LONG-BILLED MARSH WREN, *Telmatodytes palustris* (4.12-5.50), is found throughout southern Canada and the United States, and south into Mexico in winter. It makes its home among the reeds, rushes, and cattails of sloughs where the water is several inches deep, while the Short-billed may at the same time be occupying the grassy, bush-grown meadows nearer shore. The large globular nest with a hole in the side, suspended among the reed stems, is an astonishing achievement for so small a bird. The eggs are dull chocolate in color, speckled with darker.

The SHORT-BILLED MARSH WREN, *Cistothorus stellaris* (4.25-4.50), breeds in North America from southern Canada to the central United States, and winters in the southern United States. The song of the Short-bill is weaker and more attenuated than that of the Long-bill, beginning with two or three faint *chips* and running into a fine, aspirate trill which may perhaps be recalled by the syllables *chip, chip, chip, e-e-e-e-e-e*, the whole delivered in a bouncing, elastic fashion that is quite unmistakable. The nest is similar to that of the Long-billed but of finer materials; the eggs are plain white.

WINTER WREN   HOUSE WREN

CAROLINA WREN   BEWICK'S WREN

LONG-BILLED MARSH WREN   SHORT-BILLED MARSH WREN

Scale about one-half

PLATE 58

MOCKINGBIRDS, THRASHERS, AND CATBIRD (Family *Mimidae*)
AND TOWNSEND'S SOLITAIRE (Family *Turdidae*)

The members of this group are all fine singers and are, in varying degree, mockers and mimics. Their songs are loud, forcible, and varied, and that of the Mockingbird has been eulogized as superior to the performance of any other feathered songster of the world. The family *Mimidae* contains about thirty species, all of which are found only in the New World. They are related to the wrens on one side and the thrashers on the other. They live, for the most part, on or near the ground, and ascend to elevated perches chiefly when delivering their powerful, ringing songs.

The BROWN THRASHER, *Toxostoma rufum* (10.30-12), is found in North America east of the Rocky Mountains. It breeds from southern Canada to the Gulf states, and winters in the southern United States.

The arrival of the Thrasher on some mild morning in late April or early May is commonly announced by a loud and richly beautiful song, delivered in short, emphatic phrases, which at once command attention as they echo through the still leafless woods. This song is one of the finest of our open woodlands, and the great variety and richness of its notes, together with the seeming mimicry of the songs of other birds, has caused the Thrasher to be called, at times, the "Mockingbird of the North." The large, well-lined, stick nest is usually at no great height in a small tree, vine-tangled bush, brush pile, or not infrequently on the ground. The eggs are white or greenish-white, thickly speckled with reddish-brown.

The CATBIRD, *Dumetella carolinensis* (8.30-9.35), is found in North America, chiefly east of the Rocky Mountains, and south in winter as far as Panama.

The Catbird has received its unfortunate name from its unpleasant, cat-like, mewing notes, and there are not a few persons who consider this its principal utterance. Only the initiated seem to be aware that it is really one of our finest songsters. For two months or more during the nesting season the male delivers a forceful, varied, and richly musical medley, which is among the very choicest offerings of the morning and evening bird chorus. As a vocalist he has been ranked with the Mockingbird and the Thrasher and, like those birds, is an unconscious mimic, too; fragments and phrases from the songs and calls of other birds may be detected here and there throughout the performance. The nest is usually near the ground, built of sticks and weed stems, and neatly lined with rootlets, inner-bark fibers, and leaves. The eggs are plain glossy greenish-blue.

The MOCKINGBIRD, *Mimus polyglottos* (9-11), as a species is found in the southern United States from coast to coast, in northern Mexico, the Bahamas, and in the West Indies. It occurs farther north as a straggler, even to southern Canada. This famous southern songster is of rare occurrence in the upper Mississippi Valley—stray birds, more likely to be seen in the colder months. It is rather easily confused with the shrike, or still more easily with Townsend's Solitaire.

TOWNSEND'S SOLITAIRE, *Myadestes townsendi* (8), is a bird of western North America, at home in the boreal forests of western Canada and the Rocky Mountains as far south as Arizona. In winter it wanders far southward and eastward.

The Solitaire belongs with the thrushes but is placed here for direct comparison with the Mockingbird and the Catbird. It is a rare winter visitant in the upper Mississippi Valley. Taverner writes of it in its western summer home: "A bird typical of the high mountain solitudes, well named Solitaire. Its unobstrusive dull grey color, glorious song, and romantic habitat and name, surround it with an air of mystery that piques the imagination."

BROWN THRASHER   TOWNSEND'S SOLITAIRE
CATBIRD   MOCKINGBIRD

Scale about one-half

PLATE 59

THRUSHES (Family *Turdidae*)

Robins and Bluebirds are thrushes, although the plumage of the old birds does not suggest relationship with the other American thrushes. The young in the juvenal plumage, as is often the case, show the family connection more plainly, their spotted dress being more like that of the thrushes in Plate 60. The members of this family number about 600 species and are distributed throughout the world. They agree in certain characters but differ widely in general appearance and habits. The far-famed Nightingale, the Song Thrush, and the Robin Red-breast of Europe belong here, besides many others of nearly equal note. Structurally they agree in having rather small or slender bills, the upper mandible with a small notch near the tip; the outer or first wing-feather very short; the shank or tarsus smooth, without transverse scales or plates—"booted." The early young are always spotted, whatever the coloration of the adults may be. They are mostly woodland birds, feeding largely on the ground. Many are noted for their vocal ability. The North American thrushes are largely insectivorous, but they also eat worms, centipedes, snails, and spiders; and our smaller species are so fond of ants that they consume greater numbers of these little insects than any other birds except the woodpeckers. Some species, like the Robin, are fond of berries and other small fruits, and may do some damage in orchard and vineyard.

The ROBIN, *Turdus migratorius* (9-10.75), is found in summer throughout all of North America from tree-limit in the north to the Gulf of Mexico and in the mountains to southern Mexico, and in winter through Mexico to the highlands of Guatemala in Central America. Several subspecies are recognized, of which one (*T. m. propinquus*) has a darker head and a lighter back, and lacks the white spot on the tip of the outer tail feathers.

The Robin is one of the best known and most loved of all our birds. His cheery song is among the first and most welcome sounds of returning spring. Robin he is called and a Robin he is to every man, woman, and child, but, except in his confiding ways and his ruddy breast, he is little like the diminutive Old World bird, the Robin Red-breast, after which he was named by the early comers to America. The spotted breast of the young American Robin reveals its true relationship to our spotted-breasted thrushes, and its Latin name means "Migratory Thrush."

There has been considerable controversy as to the economic status of the Robin because of its serious injury, at times, to fruit crops. However, it destroys such vast numbers of injurious insects, such as cutworms, white grubs, and others, that on the whole it should be regarded as a beneficial bird.

The EASTERN BLUEBIRD, *Sialia sialis* (6.30-7.70), breeds in North America east of the Rocky Mountains, from southern Canada and Newfoundland southward. It winters chiefly south of the Ohio River and the middle Atlantic states.

The Bluebird is an early spring arrival, reaching the northern United States on the average about the middle of March, and not leaving until late fall. It is today most abundant in the well-settled country but is not at all uncommon as a summer resident in the desolate burned-over areas and windfalls of the northern forests. There it nests in holes in trees and stubs, but elsewhere it is one of the commonest box-nesting birds. The eggs are pale blue, rarely white, and unspotted. The soft, mellow warble of the Bluebird, heard at its best throughout spring and early summer, is one of the sweetest, most confiding and loving sounds in nature. The Bluebird is without serious faults and as a beneficial bird has a record equaled by few other species.

EASTERN BLUEBIRD

FEMALE   MALE

JUVENAL PLUMAGE (NESTLING)

ROBIN

MALE

FEMALE   JUVENAL PLUMAGE

Scale about one-half

PLATE 60

THRUSHES (Family *Turdidae*)

The birds assembled in this plate belong to a small group, the "Hylocichlas," which is peculiar to the Americas, breeding in North America and wintering for the most part in Central and South America. They are birds of dull plumage, forest-dwellers of shy, seclusive habits, but are possessed of wonderful, rich voices. Their songs are among the most beautiful and soul-stirring of the entire feathered tribe.

The GRAY-CHEEKED THRUSH, *Hylocichla minima* (7.50-8), is a species that breeds from northeastern Siberia across northern Alaska and Canada to Newfoundland, and in the east southward in the evergreen forests of the mountains of New England and New York, the birds of the latter region being separated as a subspecies, Bicknell's Thrush (*H. m. bicknelli*). It winters in South America as far as Peru. The gray cheeks, whitish eye-ring, and almost entire absence of buff on the breast and sides of the neck will distinguish it from the Olive-back, which it resembles closely both in appearance and in habits. On its breeding ground in the far north, and rarely during migration, it sings a song something like that of the Veery.

The WOOD THRUSH, *Hylocichla mustelina* (7.50-8.55), breeds chiefly in the deciduous forests of the eastern United States and Ontario, south to the Gulf states; it winters in southern Mexico and Central America, and occasionally in Florida. The Wood Thrush makes its home for the most part in hardwood forests, south of the evergreen forests where the Hermit prefers to dwell. The songs are very similar and easily confused. The nest is in a tree or sapling. Mud is used in its foundation and walls. The eggs are greenish-blue, unspotted.

The SWAINSON'S or OLIVE-BACKED THRUSH, *Hylocichla ustulata swainsoni* (6.35-7.75), is the more eastern of two races of a species that breeds from Alaska, northern Canada, and Newfoundland, south into the northern United States, and farther south in the mountains; it winters from southern Mexico to Peru and Argentina. The Olive-backed and Gray-cheeked thrushes migrate in company and it takes an experienced observer to distinguish between them with certainty. The song of the Swainson's resembles both the Veery and Hermit songs. The opening notes are like those of the Veery, are followed by Hermit-like refrains, and the song ends with an upward inflection instead of downward like the Veery. The nest is in a tree or on a stump; the eggs are greenish-blue, speckled with brown.

The VEERY, *Hylocichla fuscescens* (6.50-7.75), is a species that breeds in southern Canada and much of the United States, and winters in South America to Brazil. The Veery is a summer inhabitant of low, damp woodlands bordering streams and lakes. There its wonderful, ringing, whirling song, *vee-ry, vee-ry, vee-ry, vee-ry* with a wild vibrating quality, forms a considerable part of the morning and evening choir. The nest is on the ground or in a tangle of vines or upturned roots; its eggs are Robin's-egg blue, unspotted.

The HERMIT THRUSH, *Hylocichla guttata* (6.50-7.60), as a species is found throughout most of North America, breeding in the evergreen forests of the north and in high mountains; it goes south in winter as far as northern Central America. The Hermit is the divine singer of the northern evergreen forests. The song is a series of beautiful, clear, liquid refrains with something of the quality of the purest tones of a flute. It is delivered from an elevated station with deliberation, the singer pausing for a few seconds between the various phrases. It is of the quiet, serene, spiritual type, appealing chiefly to those attuned to the more subtle beauties of nature. The nest is on the ground; the eggs are greenish-blue, unspotted.

SWAINSON'S THRUSH   GRAY-CHEEKED THRUSH
VEERY   WOOD THRUSH
ADULT   ADULT
JUVENAL PLUMAGE   JUVENAL PLUMAGE

HERMIT THRUSH
ADULT
JUVENAL PLUMAGE

Scale about one-half

PLATE 61

GNATCATCHERS AND KINGLETS (Family *Sylviidae*)

This is a very numerous family, best represented in the Old World. It includes, besides the gnatcatchers and kinglets, the Old World warblers, which have ten primaries instead of nine as have the American or wood warblers. The members of this family are all small birds with short wings, tiny slender bills shorter than the head, and the upper mandible often minutely notched near the slightly hooked tip.

The gnatcatchers are peculiar to the Americas and are chiefly tropical, only two of the several species reaching North America. They are slender, flycatcher-like little birds with long, graduated tail feathers, broad at the tip instead of narrowed as in the kinglets; the long, slender shank (tarsus) is scaled instead of smooth as in the kinglets.

The kinglets are even more diminutive. They are found around the world in the Northern Hemisphere. They have soft, fluffy plumage like the tits, and are always on the move, flitting their wings constantly in their seemingly restless agitation.

The BLUE-GRAY GNATCATCHER, *Polioptila caerulea caerulea* (4.05-5), is the eastern race of a species that breeds from the northern tier of the United States south to Mexico and the Bahamas; it is uncommon in the northern United States; it winters from the southern part of the breeding range to Central America.

This dainty, trim little bird, dressed in bluish-gray and white set off by the dark wings and long black and white tail, dwells by preference and builds its exquisite, hummingbird-like nest in the treetops, where it is almost invisible from the ground below. Its song is a choice bit of bird music, soft and low but with the notes distinct and the whole a wondrous and complicated melody. The eggs are white or bluish-white, speckled with brown, chiefly at the larger end.

The RUBY-CROWNED KINGLET, *Regulus calendula* (3.75-4.60), breeds throughout northern North America, and southward in the mountains; it winters in the southern United States (north to British Columbia on the Pacific Coast) and south to Central America.

The Ruby-crown is an abundant spring and fall migrant through the United States. The trees and shrubbery are sometimes alive with them, flitting restlessly here and there with wings ever aflutter. The song is an astonishing, far-carrying, and wonderful effort to come from such a mite of a bird. It is a prolonged, varied, and deep-toned warble that, in the musical quality of certain of its strains, rivals the finest songs of some of our best and larger singers. Snatches of the beautiful spring song may be heard occasionally in the fall.

The GOLDEN-CROWNED KINGLET, *Regulus satrapa* (3.15-4.20), breeds in the evergreen forests of Canada and the northern United States, and southward in the mountains. An eastern race winters from the northern United States to the Gulf states and northeastern Mexico, and a western race as far south as Guatemala in Central America.

The Golden-crown is even tinier than the Ruby-crown and both are among the smallest of our birds. While the Ruby-crown goes farther north to nest, many Golden-crowns make their summer home south of the Canadian boundary. The partly pensile, moss nest, snugly lined with bark fiber and feathers, is usually placed high up in the thick top of a spruce. The numerous eggs, like those of the Ruby-crown, are white or creamy-white, speckled with pale brown and faint lavender. The song of the Golden-crown is a much more humble performance than the famed warble of its near relative, the Ruby-crown. It is mostly a series of faint, screeping strains with only two or three full-toned, warbling notes coming at the finish in a descending scale.

GOLDEN-CROWNED KINGLET
ADULT MALE
ADULT FEMALE

RUBY-CROWNED KINGLET
ADULT MALE
ADULT FEMALE

BLUE-GRAY GNATCATCHER
ADULT MALE

Scale about one-half

PLATE 62

WAXWINGS (Family *Bombycillidae*)

This is a small family containing only three species, one of which is found throughout the Northern Hemisphere, one in North America only, and the third in Japan, this differing from the others in having the tail tipped with rose-color instead of yellow and in lacking the sealing-wax tips on the wing feathers. They are all beautiful birds with soft, silky plumage and a conspicuous crest, present in both sexes and in the young. The adults are alike, but the young in juvenal plumage are striped and have smaller crests. The bill is short, broad at the base and notched near the decurved tip; the wings are long and pointed; the tail is rather short; and, usually, there are red sealing-wax-like appendages on the ends of the inner wing feathers, sometimes on the tail, and rarely elsewhere. These appendages are independent of sex, vary greatly in size, are often absent, and are supposed to reach their highest development with increased age or greater bodily vigor. Waxwings are songless in the true sense, uttering only rather weak, lisping, *zee*-ing notes. They nest in trees, laying greenish-blue, spotted eggs.

The BOHEMIAN WAXWING, *Bombycilla garrula* (7.40-8.75), is circumpolar in distribution, breeding in the northern portions of both the Old and New Worlds. The North American race breeds from tree-limit south to British Columbia and Alberta, and wanders south irregularly in winter into the United States and east to Nova Scotia. Allied subspecies are found in Europe and Asia.

The word elegant best describes the appearance of this handsome winter visitor from the north. When away from its northern home it is a great wanderer, whence the name "Bohemian." It is very erratic and uncertain in its appearance in the United States, now here, now there, or almost absent for several years together. In "Waxwing years" it comes in flocks, often of considerable size, and always attracts attention by its beauty and fearless ways as it searches through cities and parks for the berries upon which it feeds. Mountain ash and wolf berries are its preference. Toward spring it becomes a flycatcher, and whole flocks may be seen hawking for insects from the treetops. The flight of the Bohemian Waxwings is uneven and wayward like that of a blackbird, and when a flock alights in a treetop the birds usually sit close together, all facing the same way. The white or yellow markings on the wing, chestnut under tail-coverts, and slightly larger size distinguish this bird from the Cedar Waxwing.

The CEDAR WAXWING, *Bombycilla cedrorum* (6.50-7.52), breeds from near tree-limit in Canada south into the United States as far as northwestern California in the west and northern Georgia in the east. It winters over most of the United States and south to Cuba, Mexico, and Panama; it is accidental as far away as the British Isles.

The jaunty, top-knotted Cedar Waxwing, or Cedar Bird as it is often called, with its smooth, satiny, brown dress, rarely fails to attract the attention of the passer-by, be he bird lover or not. It is tame and unsuspicious, frequently seen, winter or summer, in cities or towns and about country dwellings, not averse to the closest inspection except in the nesting season, which is later than with most other birds. It is usually seen in flocks that go roving about, carefree and sociable and affectionate among themselves. When resting, the members of a flock are apt to sit closely snuggled together in a row, and at times may touch bills with their neighbors, first on one side, then on the other, in a manner suggesting kissing. Even more surprising, they may be seen to pass some titbit, a ripe berry most likely, from one to another all along the line and then back again several times in succession without any bird being impolite enough to eat it!

BOHEMIAN WAXWING
ADULTS

CEDAR WAXWING

JUVENAL PLUMAGE

ADULTS

Scale about one-half

PLATE 63

SHRIKES (Family *Laniidae*)

The shrikes are a numerous family, but with two exceptions are Old World birds. The two New World species are found only in North America, from Mexico northward. Shrikes are curious anomalies in the great order of perching birds, equipped as they are with the beak and instinct of a bird of prey but having toes without talons and feet too weak to hold the struggling captives that form their food. To overcome this difficulty the quarry, after being dispatched with the stout, toothed, and hooked bill, is firmly impaled on a thorn, broken twig, or the barb of a wire fence, where it can be easily dismembered and devoured at once or left for future use. Such accumulations of impaled small birds, small mammals, snakes, lizards, or large insects, have been called "shrike shambles," and give rise to the common name "Butcher Bird."

Shrikes are solitary birds, seen only singly or in pairs. Their usual notes are harsh and grating, but at rare intervals they utter a varied and voluble song of more than ordinary musical quality. The nests are bulky, warmly lined structures hidden in thorn bushes, evergreens, or among the thick lower branches of trees. The eggs are dull white, thickly spotted and blotched with shades of brown and lavender.

The NORTHERN SHRIKE, *Lanius excubitor* (9-10.75), breeds in eastern Canada and wanders south into the United States in winter.

The Northern Shrike, or Butcher Bird, enters the United States from Canada in October and advances southward during that and the following month, to remain until the latter part of April when it again crosses the International Boundary, this time northward to the breeding grounds in Canada. It is present in the United States every winter but varies greatly in numbers from season to season. It is conspicuous by its habit of perching on some commanding point of observation, and also by its hovering in the air, hawk-like, when hunting for prey over marshes and brushlands. It is bold and courageous and does not hesitate to come about farms and even to enter cities and villages in pursuit of mice and sparrows. It has been known to enter an open window and attack a caged canary, and is an unwelcome visitor to winter bird-banding stations.

The LOGGERHEAD SHRIKE or MIGRANT SHRIKE, *Lanius ludovicianus* (8.56-9.50), occurs in southern Canada and in most of the United States.

The North American shrikes are very similar in general appearance and are difficult to distinguish in the field. The greater size of the Northern, its largely light-colored under-mandible, and the fine barring of the underparts may serve to identify the adults. A shrike seen anywhere in the United States in the summertime is certainly the Loggerhead. A shrike seen in the northern states in winter is certainly the Northern. But when both are present in the transition seasons the distinction is difficult to make.

The food of the Loggerhead Shrike throughout the year consists chiefly of large ground insects rather than vertebrates; while the Northern, passing the winter in the north, is compelled to feed on small birds and mammals when the ground is snow-covered. Grasshoppers and large beetles, found impaled on barbwire fences and thorns, have been placed there by a shrike, and the pellets ejected by both old and young will usually be found to consist entirely of the indigestible parts of such insects.

NORTHERN SHRIKE

IMMATURE, FIRST WINTER

ADULT

LOGGERHEAD SHRIKE

JUVENAL PLUMAGE   ADULT

Scale about one-half

PLATE 64

VIREOS (Family *Vireonidae*)

The vireos, or greenlets as they are sometimes and not inaptly called, are found only in the New World. Of the thirty-seven species twelve occur in the United States, the others belonging to the tropics. They are small, mostly greenish, plain birds, the sexes alike and the young resembling the adults. The bill is rather stout and slightly hooked and notched. They are not as delicately built and are more deliberate in their movements than the warblers, which they somewhat resemble in appearance and habits. All our vireos build hanging, cup-shaped nests, suspended in the fork of a limb or twig. The eggs are white, spotted and speckled with dark brown and black, chiefly at the larger end. The ordinary notes are harsh and scolding, but all vireos have musical singing voices though the songs are rather weak and of short duration. The males assist in incubating the eggs and sing constantly when on the nest. Vireos feed chiefly on insects, which they glean from the leaves and twigs of the trees they inhabit or seize on the wing, flycatcher-like.

The WARBLING VIREO, *Vireo gilvus* (5-6), breeds from southern Canada throughout the United States, and winters south of the United States to Guatemala. The western and eastern birds are separated as subspecies. The Warbling Vireo is a common bird in all open woodlands. The song is a low-pitched, sweet, rolling warble ending with an upward inflection, unlike the songs of our other vireos.

The YELLOW-THROATED VIREO, *Vireo flavifrons* (5-6), breeds in eastern North America from southern Canada to the Gulf, and winters from southern Mexico to northern South America. The Yellow-throat lives and builds its nest in the treetops. Its song, like that of the Red-eye, is a series of phrases, but they are richer and more musical in quality and are delivered more slowly than those of the Red-eye.

The PHILADELPHIA VIREO, *Vireo philadelphicus* (4.50-5.10), breeds from eastern Canada south into the adjoining parts of the United States; it winters in southern Mexico and Central America. The little Philadelphia or Brotherly-love Vireo is very like the Warbling but more yellow below, and the song is broken into phrases like that of the Red-eye.

The RED-EYED VIREO, *Vireo olivaceus* (5.50-6.50), breeds over most of North America (except the southwestern states) and winters in South America to Brazil. The Red-eye is an abundant and generally distributed bird. It sings its two-phrased song incessantly from the treetops, but builds its nest among the shrubbery below. The song may be heard throughout the hot, late summer days when most bird voices are stilled.

BELL'S VIREO, *Vireo bellii* (4.75-5), is a species that breeds in the south central and the western United States, and through Mexico to Guatemala. There are several subspecies, the central United States race wintering from Mexico to Nicaragua. Bell's Vireo is a tiny bird, only a little larger than a kinglet, but its actions and song are those of a Vireo.

The SOLITARY or BLUE-HEADED VIREO, *Vireo solitarius* (5-6), breeds chiefly in the northern evergreen forests of Canada and the northern United States, south in the mountains to Guatemala in the west and to Georgia in the east; it winters from the Gulf states to Central America. It has a remarkable song of the interrupted type, with phrases quite unlike those of the other species.

The WHITE-EYED VIREO, *Vireo griseus* (4.50-5.50), is a more southerly bird not shown in the plate. It resembles the Yellow-throated Vireo but lacks the clear yellow throat and cheeks, and is distinctly smaller.

WARBLING VIREO   PHILADELPHIA VIREO
YELLOW-THROATED VIREO   RED-EYED VIREO

BELL'S VIREO   SOLITARY VIREO

Scale about one-half

PLATE 65

WOOD WARBLERS (Family *Parulidae*)

The wood, or American, warblers are small, delicately formed, often exquisitely arrayed birds, found only in the Americas. There are some 120 species, many of which are confined to the tropics. About sixty species belong to North America, all of which are migratory, many making surprisingly long journeys from their northern summer homes to winter quarters in faraway tropical lands.

The typical warbler bill is a slender, sharp-pointed, awl-like instrument for picking insects out of crevices and crannies, but a number of species have flattened bills, broad at the base, and provided with well-developed bristles around the gape, like the flycatchers. These species secure much of their food on the wing and were formerly called flycatching warblers. The Redstart and Wilson's Black-cap are conspicuous examples of this type. Few warblers are singers of any consequence, most of them having weak, high-pitched little songs of inferior musical quality. The waterthrushes, Oven-bird, and Chat are exceptions among our species. Economically the warblers are a valuable group because they are almost entirely insect gleaners. The sexes commonly are not alike after the juvenal plumage, which is often very different from that of the adults. Every bird lover finds a puzzling but interesting study in the great fall assemblages of leisurely migrating warblers made up of adults and young in obscure and unfamiliar plumages. The spring is different. Then wave after wave of these dainty little birds, dressed in their brilliant best, pass rapidly by, and the excited watcher gets the great thrill of the year.

The BLACK AND WHITE WARBLER, *Mniotilta varia* (4.55-5.50), is found in summer in North America east of the Rocky Mountains; in winter in Mexico, Central America, northern South America, Florida, the Bahamas, and West Indies. This is a warbler but it has the habits of a creeper. The song is a weak *see-see-see*. The nest is on the ground; the eggs are white, heavily spotted with brown and lavender.

The PROTHONOTARY WARBLER, *Protonotaria citrea* (5.25-5.75), is found in summer in the eastern United States (chiefly southerly), and in winter in Central America and northern South America. It breeds northward in the Mississippi Valley to southeastern Minnesota. This warbler makes its home in flooded bottomlands. The usual song is a loud, ringing *tweet, tweet, tweet,* varied with a more musical, warbled flight song. The nest is in a hole in a tree or other cavity; the eggs are pinkish-white, thickly spotted with reddish-brown and lilac.

The PARULA WARBLER, *Parula americana* (4.25-4.90), breeds in southern Canada and the eastern United States, and winters from Florida and the Bahamas south to Central America. The tiny Parula, or Blue Yellow-backed, is the daintiest of our warblers. Its song is a weak, wheezy, insect-like buzz. The nest is a marvelous hanging pouch of usnea lichen; the eggs are white, speckled with brown.

The GOLDEN-WINGED WARBLER, *Vermivora chrysoptera* (4.12-5.30), breeds chiefly in the northern part of the eastern United States, and winters in southern Central America and northern South America. It sings its weak *zee*-ing song among the treetops, but builds its nest of grasses and leaves on or near the ground; the eggs are white, speckled with brown.

The BLUE-WINGED WARBLER, *Vermivora pinus* (4.50-5), breeds in the eastern United States, and winters in southern Mexico and Central America, rarely to northern South America. The Blue-wing is an exquisite little creature. The usual song is a weak, insect-like utterance, but this may be varied and more musical. The nest is on the ground, deep cup-shaped, and built of grasses; the eggs are white, finely speckled with brown and lavender.

BLACK AND WHITE WARBLER
MALE, BREEDING ADULT
FEMALE, BREEDING ADULT
JUVENAL PLUMAGE (NESTLING)

PROTHONOTARY WARBLER
MALE, BREEDING ADULT
JUVENAL PLUMAGE (NESTLING)

PARULA WARBLER
MALE, BREEDING ADULT
FEMALE, BREEDING ADULT
JUVENAL PLUMAGE

GOLDEN-WINGED WARBLER
MALE, BREEDING ADULT
FEMALE, BREEDING ADULT

BLUE-WINGED WARBLER
MALE, BREEDING ADULT

Scale about one-half

PLATE 66

WOOD WARBLERS (Family *Parulidae*)

The TENNESSEE WARBLER, *Vermivora peregrina* (4.50-5.05), nests in evergreen forests throughout Canada and sparingly in adjoining parts of the United States; it winters from southern Mexico to northern South America.

Following a few earlier arrivals, the inconspicuous and plainly garbed little Tennessee comes in numbers with the main warbler wave about the middle of May. It might pass unnoticed among the treetops where it lives were it not for its simple, emphatic, but unmusical song, which it utters so incessantly. The nest is on the ground, sunk in the sphagnum moss, and the five to seven eggs are white, speckled with reddish-brown and lilac.

The NASHVILLE WARBLER, *Vermivora ruficapilla* (4.50-5), is a species that breeds in the evergreen forests of Canada and in the northern half of the United States, and winters chiefly in southern Mexico and northern Central America. The western race was formerly called the Calaveras Warbler.

During the month of May the Nashville forms a considerable part of the migrating warbler host and is still more abundant in the roving fall assemblages. It nests commonly in the northern forests, preferring wooded lowlands, but also makes its home in suitable places farther south. The nest is on the ground, well concealed, and the white eggs are thickly speckled with brown that forms, as is usual with warblers' eggs, a wreath about the larger end. The songs of the Nashville and Tennessee are much alike. The Nashville's song is of rather greater volume, beginning with a longer, more deliberate prelude of four or five notes, and ending in a short, rapidly weakening trill or slide; while the song of the Tennessee has a brief prelude, with a long finishing trill increasing in loudness and intensity to an abrupt ending. Both songs are more or less *chip*-ing and *zee*-ing in character and are unmusical.

The ORANGE-CROWNED WARBLER, *Vermivora celata* (4.60-5.30), is a species that breeds in the evergreen forests of most of western North America east to central Ontario, and winters in the southern United States (chiefly coastwise) in Mexico and northern Central America.

The very plainly dressed Orange-crown is one of the early warblers, coming about the first of May, soon after the first "Myrtle wave." The nest is on the ground and the eggs are similar to those of the Nashville and Tennessee. The song is described as resembling that of the Chipping Sparrow but higher-pitched and ending on a rising scale. The Orange-crown is not an easy bird to place, especially in the fall when mingled with other dull-colored migrants. The pale yellow underparts with a few indistinct olive streaks must serve to separate it from the Nashville and Tennessee. Rarely can the chestnut crown patch of the Nashville or the rusty-orange patch of the Orange-crown be seen in the field.

The CAPE MAY WARBLER, *Dendroica tigrina* (4.70-5.65), breeds throughout much of Canada east of the Rocky Mountains, and in the extreme northern parts of New England; it winters in the Bahamas and the West Indies.

The Cape May is one of our choicest and most beautiful warblers. The male, in his rich and varied plumage, is a conspicuous and unusually attractive bird. The more plainly marked female and the fall young are difficult birds to place, but the yellow rump may be a guide after eliminating the Myrtle and Magnolia. The Cape May passes with the main warbler wave in mid-May, to nest amid the evergreen forests of Canada. The nest is usually high up in a spruce tree, and the eggs are white, speckled and blotched with reddish-brown and a few dots of dark brown or black. The song is an unhurried *zee-zee-zee-zee,* of little musical quality.

TENNESSEE WARBLER

NASHVILLE WARBLER   BREEDING ADULT

MALE, BREEDING ADULT   IMMATURE, FALL

JUVENAL PLUMAGE (NESTLING)

ORANGE-CROWNED WARBLER

MALE, BREEDING ADULT

IMMATURE, FALL

CAPE MAY WARBLER

FEMALE, BREEDING ADULT   MALE, BREEDING ADULT

IMMATURE, FALL

Scale about one-half

PLATE 67

WOOD WARBLERS (Family *Parulidae*)

The MAGNOLIA WARBLER, *Dendroica magnolia* (4.35-5.10), breeds in the pine forests of Canada east from Mackenzie, and in the northern United States east from Minnesota, south in the Alleghany Mountains to the Virginias; it winters from the eastern coast of Mexico to Panama.

The Magnolia, or more appropriately the Black and Yellow Warbler, is a handsome little fellow that passes north in the spring to dwell for the summer among the spruces of the north woods. The nest is usually in a small evergreen; the eggs are dull white, spotted with brown and lavender. The usual song is a simple little warble of three or four double notes, musical and somewhat fuller and more pleasing than the average warbler song.

The YELLOW WARBLER, *Dendroica petechia* (4.75-5.25), in one or another of several subspecies breeds throughout nearly all of North America, and winters chiefly in Central and South America as far as Brazil and Peru.

The simple but pleasing little ditty of the Yellow Warbler, or "Summer Yellow-bird," is heard wherever there are woods or brushlands. The neat, compactly made nest is usually in a low bush, and the four or five eggs are bluish-white, speckled with brown forming a wreath about the larger end.

The BLACK-THROATED BLUE WARBLER, *Dendroica caerulescens* (4.82-5.50), breeds in the evergreen forests of the northern United States as far west as Minnesota, and in southern Canada to Manitoba, south in the mountains to Pennsylvania; it winters chiefly in the Bahamas and West Indies.

The Black-throated Blue is one of the rarer warblers in the Midwest. It comes with the main warbler wave in mid-May. The female, so unlike her mate, is easily overlooked, the white spot on the wing being almost the only identification mark. The nest may be looked for in the northern pine forests. It is usually not far from the ground in a small bush or shrub, is bulky for a warbler, and contains in its structure bits of rotten wood. The eggs are dull or greenish-white, marked with reddish-brown and lavender. The song is a simple, unmusical *"whee-a, whee-a, whee-a, whee-ee,"* increasing in volume and force to the end.

KIRTLAND'S WARBLER, *Dendroica kirtlandii* (5.30-6), so far as is known breeds only in a limited area in the jack-pine region of the northern part of the lower peninsula of Michigan, and winters in the Bahamas. In migration it has been taken as a straggler in Ontario, Illinois, Missouri, and Minnesota.

The strange manner of occurrence of Kirtland's Warbler in only a restricted area in both the north and the south surround it with special interest. It is somewhat terrestrial in habit and a tail-wagger like the Palm Warbler. The nest is on the ground; the eggs are white, spotted with reddish- and dark-brown. The song is described as a loud, forcible, and musical *chip-chip-che-chee chee-r-r-r,* or at times a *wichy-chee-chee-chee-r-r.*

The MYRTLE WARBLER, *Dendroica coronata* (5-6), occurs throughout most of North America, breeding in the evergreen forests of Alaska, Canada, and the northern United States east of the Great Plains; it winters chiefly from the southern United States south to the West Indies, Mexico, and Panama; north to Oregon on the Pacific coast.

The Myrtle is the hardiest of the warblers and the first to arrive in the Northland in the spring, usually while the ice and snow still linger. Its summer home is in the northern pine forests. Of the great numbers that pass by comparatively few stop to nest south of the Canadian boundary. The usual song consists of a few hurried screeping notes—*weech, weech, weech*—followed occasionally by one or two lower, more liquid, pleasing notes. The nest is in an evergreen tree; the eggs are white, speckled with reddish-brown and lilac.

MAGNOLIA WARBLER   YELLOW WARBLER
MALE, BREEDING ADULT   MALE, BREEDING ADULT
IMMATURE, FALL   FEMALE, BREEDING ADULT

BLACK-THROATED BLUE WARBLER
MALE, BREEDING ADULT

FEMALE, BREEDING ADULT

KIRTLAND'S WARBLER   MYRTLE WARBLER
MALE, BREEDING ADULT   IMMATURE, FALL

MALE, BREEDING ADULT

Scale about one-half

PLATE 68

WOOD WARBLERS (Family *Parulidae*)

The BLACK-THROATED GREEN WARBLER, *Dendroica virens* (4.35-5.30), breeds in the more southern parts of Canada east from Alberta, in Newfoundland, and south in the United States to the central states and northern New Jersey, in the mountains to South Carolina, Georgia, and Alabama; it winters in Mexico and Central America.

The male Black-throated Green easily takes rank among the daintiest and prettiest of the warbler group. It is an early arrival, reaching the northern states in early May ahead of the main warbler wave. In nesting time it seeks the seclusion of great forests, either deciduous or evergreen. Its slow, lazy song of several gliding notes comes from high up among the leafy foliage—*zee, zee, zu, ze,* the third note slurred upward and then downward—a sweet, drowsy little song that cannot be mistaken for anything else. The nest of fine twigs and bark fibers is out on the limb of a tree two to forty feet from the ground; the eggs are white, thickly spotted with brown and lilac.

The CERULEAN WARBLER, *Dendroica cerulea* (4-5), breeds in the eastern United States from the southern parts of the northernmost states and from southern Ontario south to the Gulf states; it winters in South America south to Peru.

The beautiful little Cerulean is a southern species that has been extending its range northward in recent years by way of the Mississippi bottomlands. In nesting time it is a dweller in the tops of the tallest trees where its uniform coloration and diminutive size make it a very difficult bird to locate and identify except with the strongest glasses. It places its tiny nest saddled on a spreading branch and stuccoed with bits of lichen and wasp's nest. The eggs are pale bluish- or greenish-white, speckled with reddish-brown and lavender. The usual song is an unpretentious and unmusical effort of several *tse*-ing notes, ending in a longer trill on a rising inflection (Lynds Jones). At times it utters, also, a few soft warbling notes.

The PINE WARBLER, *Dendroica pinus* (4.95-5.75), breeds in eastern North America from the pine forests of southern Alberta to the Gulf states, the Bahamas, and Haiti; it winters chiefly in the southern United States and northeastern Mexico. The resident birds of southern Florida, the Bahamas, and Haiti are separated as closely allied subspecies.

The plainly colored Pine Warbler is well named, for it spends its entire existence, with the exception of the time consumed in migration, among pine trees. In the north it prefers the more open jack-pine forests where its fine, rattling trill, not very unlike that of the Junco, may be heard almost constantly. The nest is usually high up on a horizontal limb of a pine tree, well out toward the tip, and the four or five eggs are white, spotted with brown forming a wreath around the larger end.

The BLACKBURNIAN WARBLER, *Dendroica fusca* (4.47-5.50), breeds in the coniferous forests of southern Canada east from Manitoba and of the northern United States, south in the mountains to Georgia; it winters from southern Mexico (Yucatan) south to Peru.

The beautifully arrayed Blackburnian Warbler, appearing like an exquisite exotic from the tropics, reaches its summer home in the northern pinelands with the mid-May warbler wave. The brilliant orange-red throat of the male and the orange head-markings, framed in black, never fail to elicit the admiration of the bird lover. It lives in summer among the tops of the tallest pines and spruces, where its weak, thin *wee-see, tsee, tsee,* which passes for a song, barely reaches the ear of the listener below. The nest is placed high up in an evergreen tree, usually far out on a spreading limb, and contains three or four dull white eggs, marked with reddish-brown spots and blotches.

BLACK-THROATED GREEN WARBLER   CERULEAN WARBLER
MALE, BREEDING ADULT   MALE, BREEDING ADULT
FEMALE, BREEDING ADULT   FEMALE, BREEDING ADULT

BLACKBURNIAN WARBLER
PINE WARBLER   FEMALE, BREEDING ADULT
BREEDING ADULT   MALE, BREEDING ADULT
IMMATURE, FALL   IMMATURE, FALL

Scale about one-half

PLATE 69

WOOD WARBLERS (Family *Parulidae*)

The CHESTNUT-SIDED WARBLER, *Dendroica pensylvanica* (4.60-5.25), breeds in southern Canada east from Saskatchewan, and south in the United States to the central states and northern New Jersey, in the mountains south to South Carolina and Tennessee; it winters in Central America.

The pretty little Chestnut-sided Warbler lives amid surroundings almost identical with those chosen by the Yellow Warbler. The songs also are so similar to the untrained ear that they may easily be confused, so that a sight of the bird is necessary to make the identification certain. Formerly the Chestnut-side was almost as abundant as the Yellow Warbler in all open woodlands and brushlands, but in recent years it is much reduced in numbers south of the open glades and clearings of the northern forests. The nest and eggs, in location and details, are almost exactly like those of the Yellow Warbler.

The plumage of the young birds, when they leave the nest, is very unlike any later dress. They are dark brown above, faintly streaked with black and a paler brown below, fading to grayish or dull white on throat and abdomen. This juvenal dress is soon changed for the fall plumage shown in the plate.

The BLACK-POLL WARBLER, *Dendroica striata* (5-5.75), breeds in Alaska, Canada, and Newfoundland, in northern Michigan and Maine, and in the mountains of New York, Vermont, and New Hampshire. It winters in northern South America.

Following a few scattered earlier arrivals the main spring movement of the Black-poll comes toward the end of the warbler migration. It seeks by preference the treetops, and as the leaves are then appearing it is almost lost amid the early foliage. This is especially true of the greenish, dull-colored female, which blends so closely with her surroundings. It is often early June before the last of the migrants have left for their Canadian summer homes. The nest is not far up in spruces or other evergreens; the eggs are white or whitish, speckled with brown and lilac.

The Black-poll has a weak, unmusical, and exceedingly unpretentious song, consisting of a series of fine notes, usually all alike and all uttered on the same pitch, the voice gliding quickly from one to another, increasing in intensity to the middle and then fading away.

The BAY-BREASTED WARBLER, *Dendroica castanea* (5-6), breeds in the coniferous forests of Canada east from Alberta, in Newfoundland, and in the northern United States; it winters from Guatemala to Colombia.

The Bay-breasted Warbler is arrayed in rather somber colors but is of special interest to the bird watcher because of its comparative rarity. It is one of the largest of the warblers like the Black-poll, with which species it is frequently associated in migration. But, unlike the Black-poll, a considerable number of Bay-breasts remain to pass the summer and nest in the evergreen forests of the northern United States. The nest is not far from the ground in an evergreen tree and is rather bulky and loosely constructed. The eggs are pale greenish-gray to pale blue and are heavily marked with reddish-brown and lavender.

The Bay-breast, like most of the warblers, has several more or less distinct songs, all of which are thin-voiced and lisping. The most usual has been represented by the syllables *tse-chee, tse-chee, tse-chee, tse-chee, tse-chee,* with little or no variation in the notes. The young fall birds are very different from their attractive spring parents, being clothed in dull yellow, olive, and gray, commonly with a buffy tinge on the sides and under tail-coverts, which is almost the only distinction between them and their traveling companions, the young Black-polls.

CHESTNUT-SIDED WARBLER

MALE, BREEDING ADULT

IMMATURE, FALL   FEMALE, BREEDING ADULT

BLACK-POLL WARBLER

MALE, BREEDING ADULT   IMMATURE, FALL

FEMALE, BREEDING ADULT

BAY-BREASTED WARBLER

IMMATURE, FALL   FEMALE, BREEDING ADULT

MALE, BREEDING ADULT

Scale about one-half

PLATE 70

WOOD WARBLERS (Family *Parulidae*)

WILSON'S WARBLER, *Wilsonia pusilla* (4.25-5.10), occurs throughout North America, breeding chiefly in evergreen forests north of the United States and farther south in high mountains; it winters from Mexico to Central America.

Wilson's Warbler, or "Wilson's Black-cap," is a dainty, sprightly little bird that lives chiefly in the lower growth, sings a short, weak, lisping song of little character, and builds a nest on the ground amid the northern pines. The eggs are white, thickly marked with reddish-brown and lavender.

The YELLOW-BREASTED CHAT, *Icteria virens* (6.75-7.50), breeds locally in southern Canada and the northern United States, becoming more widespread in the south; it winters from southern Texas to Central America. The Chat is the largest of the warblers. The song is a medley of whistles, clucks, and strange notes, some of them borrowed, which comes from the dense thickets in which the Chat dwells or is delivered while the bird hovers and tumbles about in the air above its home. The nest is near the ground, large, and coarsely built; and the eggs are white, evenly marked with rufous and brown.

The CANADA WARBLER, *Wilsonia canadensis* (5-5.75), breeds in the coniferous forests of southern Canada east from Alberta, and in the northern United States, south in the mountains to Georgia and Tennessee; it winters chiefly in South America to Peru. The Canada, or "Necklaced," Warbler is a lover of the open glades or second-growth areas of the northern forests. Here it makes its home and builds its nest on or near the ground, laying eggs that are white, marked with rufous and brown. The song is a simple lay but vigorous and ringing in quality and it attracts and fixes the attention. It has been aptly likened to the syllables *rup-it-chee, rup-it-chee, rup-it-chee, rup-it-chit-it-lit.*

NORTHERN WATERTHRUSH, *Seiurus noveboracensis* (5.50-6.50), breeds in the evergreen forests of Canada and the northern United States, and winters in the Bahamas, West Indies, Florida, and through Mexico to northern South America. It seeks the margins of woodland pools or streams, where it walks daintily along from one elevation to another, swaying and tilting its tail in unison with its mincing steps. It is shy and elusive and if possible avoids observation. But the clear, liquid, emphatic song of several notes, carrying far through the forest, will disclose its presence though the singer may be difficult to see. There is also a flight or passion song uttered as the bird vaults up above the treetops. The nest is on the ground or among the roots of an upturned tree; the eggs are white, marked with brown and lavender.

The LOUISIANA WATERTHRUSH, *Seiurus motacilla* (5.75-6.40), breeds in the eastern United States (chiefly southward), and winters chiefly from Mexico to northern South America. The Louisiana or Southern Waterthrush is a more southern species than the Northern but is extending its range northward and is now a nesting bird in southeastern Minnesota, though as yet uncommon. The Northern makes its summer home in the northern evergreen forests, while the Louisiana nests along wooded streams farther south. The Louisiana, like the Northern, is a dainty walker, a graceful tail-swayer, and is fully as shy and elusive. The songs are similar but they can be distinguished by a trained ear. The nests and eggs are also similar.

WILSON'S WARBLER
ADULT MALE
ADULT FEMALE

YELLOW-BREASTED CHAT
ADULT

CANADA WARBLER
ADULT FEMALE
ADULT MALE

NORTHERN WATERTHRUSH
ADULT

LOUISIANA WATERTHRUSH
ADULT

Scale about one-half

PLATE 71

WOOD WARBLERS (Family *Parulidae*)

The CONNECTICUT WARBLER, *Oporornis agilis* (5.20-6), breeds in southern Canada from Alberta to Ontario, and immediately south of the International Boundary from northern Minnesota to northern Michigan; it winters in northern South America. The spring migration northward is chiefly through the Mississippi Valley, the fall migration southward chiefly east of the Alleghanies.

The Connecticut Warbler is usually seen alone, rarely if ever mingling with other species. It nests usually amid evergreen surroundings, choosing for its home spruce and tamarack bogs, but in Alberta it has been found nesting among poplars on the uplands. The nest is on the ground, well concealed among northern plants. The eggs are white, speckled and spotted with purplish-brown, chiefly about the larger end. So shy and elusive is this bird in its nesting haunts that its presence would rarely be suspected were it not for its loud and characteristic song, which has been likened to the syllables *freecher-here, freecher-here, freecher-here, freech.* Like the waterthrushes and Oven-bird it is a walker, but lacks the tail-wagging mannerism. The presence of the distinct, white eye-ring is the chief field mark distinguishing the Connecticut from the Mourning Warbler.

The MOURNING WARBLER, *Oporornis philadelphia* (4.90-5.75), breeds in southern Canada east from Alberta, and immediately south of the International Boundary from northern Minnesota eastward, south to West Virginia in the mountains; in migration it is found mainly west of the Alleghanies. It winters in Central America and northern South America.

The Mourning Warbler makes its home in the northern evergreen forests, both on the uplands and in the wooded lowlands. It selects, especially, burned-over areas, where it conceals its nest in a grassy tussock in the tangled second-growth below. From a perch on a dead tree above the male chants, over and over again, his simple song of four or five varied notes. The eggs are white, sparsely marked with brown and lilac-gray, chiefly about the larger end. The young birds in the fall are rather nondescript, and as they have a noticeable light eye-ring are easily confused with the Connecticut.

The YELLOW-THROAT, *Geothlypis trichas* (4.40-5.75), in one or another of its numerous races occurs throughout nearly all of North America, and winters from the southern United States and the California coast south to the Bahamas, West Indies, and through Mexico to Costa Rica. This is the "Maryland Yellow-throat" of the older books.

Rare indeed would it be to find a bushy meadow by brook or lake-side where the cheery and forcible ditty—*witch-i-te, witch-i-te, witch-i-te*—of the beautiful and animated little male Yellow-throat would not greet the late spring and early summer visitor. No member of the warbler family is more generally distributed or represented by a greater number of individuals during the nesting season. Occasionally a pair selects a woody spot on the uplands, but almost always it dwells in or beside the marsh or swamp. The usual song, as indicated above, is by some individuals replaced by a *tse-sweet, tse-sweet, tse-sweet, sweet, sweet, sweet.* At infrequent intervals the male may spring quickly upward fifteen or twenty feet above his place of concealment and, with quivering wings, give utterance to a love or flight song that is a varied, rapid warble quite unlike the usual effort, ending with a quick dive back to cover. The nest is on or near the ground, supported by the surrounding vegetation, built externally of coarse grasses, deeply cupped and usually well concealed. The eggs are white, marked with various shades of brown, chiefly about the larger end.

CONNECTICUT WARBLER

FEMALE, BREEDING ADULT   MALE, BREEDING ADULT

IMMATURE

MOURNING WARBLER

MALE, BREEDING ADULT

FEMALE, BREEDING ADULT

IMMATURE, FALL

YELLOW-THROAT

FEMALE, BREEDING ADULT

MALE, BREEDING ADULT   IMMATURE, FALL

Scale about one-half

PLATE 72

WOOD WARBLERS (Family *Parulidae*)

The AMERICAN REDSTART, *Setophaga ruticilla* (4.60-5.75), breeds throughout southern Canada, Newfoundland, and most of the United States, and winters in the West Indies and from central Mexico to northern South America.

The pretty little Redstart is a common and generally distributed bird throughout all the woodlands of this region though it may easily be overlooked because of its diminutive size and feeble voice. It is imbued with a spirit of unceasing activity and its tiny little body is ever in a state of fluttering agitation. The drooping, half-spread wings, expanded tail, and generally loose and fluffy plumage, with an occasional carelessly uttered ditty, give to the little sprite an air of abandon and gaiety that marks it among its fellows. Among a variety of songs the most common is a weak, unmusical effort, delivered without ceremony as it flits about. It has been represented by the syllables *che che che che-pa*. The female sings also, and the young male is in voice the first spring, before it has acquired its full plumage. The nest is a pretty affair several feet up in a small tree or vine. The eggs are dull white, marked with brown and lilac, chiefly about the larger end.

The PALM WARBLER, *Dendroica palmarum* (4.50-5.50), breeds in Canada east from Mackenzie, in Newfoundland, and in the coniferous forests of the northern United States east from northern Minnesota; it winters in the Bahamas, the West Indies, the southern United States west to Louisiana, and in Mexico.

The Palm, or Yellow Red-poll, Warbler is seen most frequently on the ground where it hops actively about, bobbing or dipping its tail in a most characteristic manner. It is an early arrival in the spring, coming either with or shortly after the Myrtle. It passes quickly on to make its summer home among the northern pines. The nest is on or very near the ground, frequently sunk to the rim in a sphagnum hummock in a spruce-tamarack bog. It is commonly well lined with feathers. The eggs are white, well marked with brown and lavender, chiefly about the larger end. The Palm is a constant singer, but the song is a simple, weak trill—one of the humblest of warbler songs.

The OVEN-BIRD, *Seiurus aurocapillus* (5.40-6.50), breeds throughout Canada east from Mackenzie, in Newfoundland, and in most of the United States east of the Rocky Mountains; it winters in the Bahamas, the West Indies, on the Gulf coast, and south through Mexico to northern South America.

The Oven-bird is a plain, modest little creature, shy and suspicious in the presence of man; a lover of the deep woods, from the protecting shade of which it rarely ventures; often heard, seldom seen; a graceful walker instead of a hopper; a gentle tail-bobber like the waterthrushes; and possessed of a voice and an exuberance of spirit during the courting time not excelled by any of its fellows.

The ordinary song of the Oven-bird is an emphatic, ringing series of notes beginning low and deliberately, and increasing in volume, intensity, and rapidity until it ends with a vigor that sends the last note echoing among the treetops. John Burroughs rendered the song thus: TEACHER, TEACHER, TEACHER, TEACHER, TEACHER, and gave to the singer the now well-known name of "Teacher Bird." The ardent courting male has another, more wonderful song, a passion song, delivered usually as the bird hovers in the air above the treetops. The nest is on the ground, well concealed and arched over like a Dutch oven, whence the name Oven-bird. The eggs are white, marked with brown, chiefly at the larger end.

AMERICAN REDSTART

MALE, FIRST BREEDING PLUMAGE   FEMALE, BREEDING ADULT

MALE, BREEDING ADULT

PALM WARBLER

BREEDING ADULT   JUVENAL PLUMAGE

OVEN-BIRD

JUVENAL PLUMAGE (NESTLING)   BREEDING ADULT

Scale about one-half

PLATE 73

MEADOWLARKS, BLACKBIRDS, AND ALLIES (Family *Icteridae*)

This large family is peculiar to the New World. There are nearly a hundred species, which differ greatly in external appearance and habits. Included in the family are such apparently diverse forms as the blackbirds, the orioles, the Bobolink, the cowbirds, and the tropical oropendolas and caciques, most of the species being found only in the tropics. About twenty species occur north of Mexico. The members of this group are nine-primaried birds with stout, more or less conical bills not notched or hooked at the end, the lower mandible angled or decurved at the base as it is in the sparrow family. The ridge of the bill (culmen) is usually prolonged backward onto the forehead, dividing the feather outline at the base of the bill. The species vary greatly in habits, some being strictly terrestrial, others arboreal. The former are walkers, the latter hoppers. Except the orioles and meadowlarks, the North American species are highly gregarious, assembling in large flocks, the sexes separately, and migrating at different times. The sexes differ in plumage, the female being more plainly colored and generally smaller than the male. The food habits of the blackbirds are such that they may at times do serious damage to crops, and for this reason they are not generally protected by law.

The BOBOLINK, *Dolichonyx oryzivorus* (6.30-8), breeds in southern Canada east from southeastern British Columbia, and from northeastern California east through the United States to New Jersey; it winters chiefly in southern Brazil and neighboring countries. The main migration route is from Florida to Cuba, to Jamaica, and across the Caribbean Sea—the "Bobolink route." The striking garb of the male Bobolink, and still more his joyous, bubbling song, have made him well known and a universal favorite in his summer home in the north. His praises have been sung by many writers, both in prose and poetry. He lives with his plainly colored spouse in meadows and lowlands, where the nest is deeply hidden in the thick grass. The eggs are dull white, thickly marked and often clouded with brown, gray, and lilac. As summer wanes the male changes his fine dress to one closely resembling that of the female, and in this garb both he and his mates are known as the "Rice-bird" and "Reed-bird." In his faraway winter home in Brazil he again undergoes a complete molt back into the summer attire, which, however, is veiled by rusty feather edgings. These wear off gradually so that by the time he reaches his summer home he is once more the gay Bobolink of the northern meadows.

The WESTERN MEADOWLARK, *Sturnella neglecta* (8.50-10.12), breeds in southern Canada west from Manitoba, and in the United States chiefly west of the Mississippi Valley, south to northern Mexico; it winters in the southern part of its range. The Western Meadowlark is an abundant and attractive feature of the western plains. Its wild, pure, clear whistle, carrying far over the great open stretches, has a richness of tone and a ringing quality not possessed by any forest-encompassed bird. The arched-over nest is skillfully concealed in the dense grass, and the white eggs are speckled all over with brown and purplish.

The EASTERN MEADOWLARK, *Sturnella magna* (8.50-10.12), in one or another of three subspecies occupies North America east of the range of the western species. The song of the Eastern Meadowlark is shorter, thinner, weaker, and higher pitched than that of the Western, is much less musical, and has less carrying quality. The call notes are even more unlike. Those of the Western are an emphatic *chuck* often followed by a rolling *b-r-r-r,* very different from the sharp, metallic *yert* of the Eastern. The differences in the plumage are scarcely discernible in the field, and these different vocal utterances are the only safe guide in distinguishing between the species. The nest and eggs are alike in the two species.

BOBOLINK

MOLTING MALE   MALE, BREEDING ADULT

JUVENAL PLUMAGE (NESTLING)   FEMALE (AND FALL MALE)

WESTERN MEADOWLARK   EASTERN MEADOWLARK

ADULT MALE   ADULT MALE

JUVENAL PLUMAGE

Scale about one-half

PLATE 74

BLACKBIRDS (Family *Icteridae*)

The YELLOW-HEADED BLACKBIRD, *Xanthocephalus xanthocephalus* (8.70-11.10), breeds from western Canada south to northern Mexico and east to Wisconsin and Indiana; it winters in the southwestern United States east to Louisiana, and south to southern Mexico.

The Yellow-headed Blackbird is preeminently a native of the Great Plains. Wherever it breeds it congregates in colonies, and these assemblages are often of vast proportions. It is very loyal to its homesite, returning year after year even though the surroundings may undergo great and uncongenial changes, and deserting it only with the drying up of the marsh. The Yellow-head is very closely restricted to its special nesting haunts. Since members of each colony go in the spring directly to their particular rendezvous and wander but a little way into the surrounding country until after the completion of the breeding period, they are easily overlooked if their nesting sloughs are not numerous or their homes not actually invaded.

The song of the male Yellow-head, if song it may be called, is a most remarkable, un-musical, and un-bird-like effort. At a time of the year when most other birds are singing finished nuptial songs, however humble, this fine fellow, perched aloft on a cluster of sway-ing reed stems, is straining every nerve in an attempt that results, after a few harsh but fairly promising preliminary notes, in a seemingly painful choking spell, which terminates in a long-drawn, rasping squeal that is nothing short of harrowing. Even the ordinary call note is a hoarse, rattling croak that suggests a chronic sore throat. The voice of the female is less harsh. The typical nest is a large, firm, inverted-cone-shaped, basket-like affair, usually suspended among the rigid stems of last year's reeds. The eggs vary from dull grayish-white to pale olive, and are thickly speckled or blotched with shades of brown and gray, and usually faintly penciled and dotted with black or dark brown.

As an economic factor the Yellow-headed Blackbird plays about the same role as the Red-wing; but the fact that it is much less numerous and much more restricted in its general range renders it of less importance than the latter enormously abundant and widely distributed species. It is, however, a large, sturdy, and voracious bird, and locally its cohorts are often legion, so that the food levies it may make upon the farmer's crops are by no means trifling.

The RED-WINGED BLACKBIRD, *Agelaius phoeniceus* (7.50-9.50), occurs over nearly all of North America and most of Mexico. The more northern-breeding birds winter in the southern breeding range.

Wherever there are marshes or sloughs or low-lying wet meadows, there the Red-wing is almost certain to be found. It is, perhaps, the most abundant and widely distrib-uted native bird in North America. The male, with his gorgeous scarlet epaulets and his cheery, musical *o-ka-lee* sounded over the still frozen northern marshes in early spring, may receive a joyous welcome from the bird lover, but he and his song are apt to arouse very different feelings in the farmer. During seeding time, later when the corn and grain are in the milk, and still later when the small grains are being harvested, the great flocks of Red-wings, augmented by other members of the family, take a toll from these crops far too heavy to be complacently borne by the tiller of the soil. At other times the Red-wings, and blackbirds in general, consume large quantities of weed seeds and injurious insects; but, beneficial as this may be, the plundered farmer can hardly be expected to accept it as a worth-while recompense. The grass nest is commonly suspended among rushes and reeds, but may be in willows or upland shrubs. The eggs are bluish-white, marked with spots and zigzag lines of black and purplish.

YELLOW-HEADED BLACKBIRD

MALE, FULLY ADULT   MALE, FIRST BREEDING PLUMAGE

JUVENAL PLUMAGE (NESTLING)   FEMALE

RED-WINGED BLACKBIRD

MALE, FULLY ADULT   MALE, FIRST BREEDING PLUMAGE

FEMALE

Scale about one-half

PLATE 75

ORIOLES (Family *Icteridae*)

The American orioles are a numerous group found throughout the temperate and tropical regions of the New World, most abundantly in the tropics. The males are mostly birds of brilliant hues, while the females and young are much plainer. They are tree-dwellers, building woven, pendant nests. On the ground they hop, instead of walking like the other members of the family. They are chiefly beneficial birds, living largely on caterpillars and other insects. The garden vegetables that they take, such as peas and small fruits, form only a small part of their diet. It is chiefly the owners of small gardens, where the supply is limited, who suffer serious loss.

The ORCHARD ORIOLE, *Icterus spurius* (6-7.25), breeds from southern Manitoba and Ontario and the northern United States east from the Dakotas, south to the Gulf states and central Mexico; it winters from southern Mexico to northern Colombia.

The Orchard Oriole prefers open woodlands and isolated groves, such as the tree claims on the western prairies. It makes its presence known by a rich and gushing song very different from the disconnected, flute-like phrases of the Baltimore Oriole. It may sing while concealed in the thick foliage, but more often during its passage from tree to tree, or it may sing a rapid, ecstatic flight song while hovering in the air above some treetop. The nest is neatly woven of green grass and is suspended in an upright crotch among the branches of a tree, usually at a height of ten to forty feet. The eggs are bluish-white, marked with irregular lines and streaks and a few dots of brown and lavender. The nest is often in the same tree with a kingbird's nest, an unusual toleration on the part of the testy and quarrelsome "King of Birds."

The male Orchard Oriole breeds in two quite different plumages. The second year he is dressed nearly like the female except for the possession of a black throat, but before the next season he has donned the black and chestnut suit of the mature male. The female in choosing a mate must decide between these two very different appearing suitors.

The BALTIMORE ORIOLE, *Icterus galbula* (7-8), breeds in North America east of the Rocky Mountains from southern Canada to the Gulf states; it winters from southern Mexico to Colombia.

The male Baltimore Oriole, arrayed in his best, occupies a place among the most beautiful of our birds. The name "Golden Robin" does but scant justice to the brilliant orange-red in which many of the older birds are dressed, and when, as occasionally happens, this is replaced by a vivid, intense blood-red, he vies with the Scarlet Tanager in radiant beauty. The nest, constructed entirely by the female, is a deep, marvelously woven, purse-like structure, suspended among the outermost twigs of a swaying branch and bearing at its bottom a secondary nest of plant-down and other soft materials. The eggs are white, marked with irregular scrolls and dots of brown, black, and lavender.

The song consists of loud, clear, flute-like, disconnected phrases uttered as the bird moves about among the treetops. There is much variation in the songs of both the same and of different birds. Certain individuals have notes peculiar to them alone, which may serve to identify them as they return each year. A spring male has been heard to utter incessantly a clear-cut *Chewink* call. A frequent note is a loud and distinct *peter, peter, peter*. Nestling Baltimore Orioles are the crybabies of the bird world, uttering all day long from the treetops a monotonous, incessant *teé-dee-dee, teé-dee-dee,* while waiting to be fed. The male, in common with numerous other birds, has a second song period in late August and September, after the molt is over.

ORCHARD ORIOLE

BREEDING MALE, FULLY ADULT

FEMALE   MALE, FIRST BREEDING PLUMAGE

BALTIMORE ORIOLE

FEMALE

MALE, BREEDING ADULT

IMMATURE MALE, FALL

Scale about one-half

PLATE 76

BLACKBIRDS (Family *Icteridae*)

The RUSTY BLACKBIRD, *Euphagus carolinus* (8.20-9.75), breeds in Alaska, east through northern and central Canada to the Atlantic, and south into northern New York and northern New England; it winters chiefly in the southern United States east of the Great Plains.

In the spring, usually in April, it is not uncommon to see a group of tall, leafless trees filled with a great mixed flock of Rusties, Red-wings, and perhaps a few Brewer's Blackbirds, all singing in unison, each bird striving to do its very best. The resulting chorus is audible for a quarter of a mile or more. The effect is that of an immense number of tinkling sleigh bells with an undertone like the creaking of wheels on frozen snow. It is a pleasing and not unmusical performance and the birds seem always to be having the very best time imaginable. The nest is in bushes or small trees and the eggs are like those of Brewer's.

BREWER'S BLACKBIRD, *Euphagus cyanocephalus* (8.75-10.15), breeds in southern Canada west from Manitoba, and south throughout the United States west from the Mississippi Valley, locally farther east; it winters in the southern part of its breeding range, south to Guatemala.

Brewer's Blackbird is one of several western species that are extending their breeding ranges eastward. Nesting colonies are now to be found in localities where twenty-five years ago it was unknown. It is a meadow-loving and aggressive bird and it is to be feared that it may displace the Bobolink, which selects similar homesites. Brewer's returns earlier than the Bobolink and is on the ground before that far-traveler arrives. In the Brewer's original western home the nest is commonly in bushes and small trees, but these immigrants have taken to nesting on the ground, rarely elsewhere. The eggs are dull white, so thickly marked with brown and blackish that the ground color is obscured.

The COMMON GRACKLE, *Quiscalus quiscula* (11-13.50), nests over most of temperate North America east of the Rockies, and winters chiefly in the southern part of its range. The bronze back color of midwestern birds gave them the older name "Bronzed Grackle," while the more purplish sheen on the eastern birds gave them the name "Purple Grackle."

The handsome Common Grackle, or "Crow Blackbird," is one of the most common native lawn birds. Throughout the summer, and especially in the fall, the Grackle may be seen striding rapidly about city lawns and the grassy stretches in parks, gleaning insects from the surface, grubs from beneath the surface, scattered seeds, fallen berries and acorns, and, in fact, anything edible, for the Crow Blackbird is not a fastidious feeder. Lake shores, riverbanks, and mud flats have also a special appeal. Here it patrols the water's edge, often wading body-deep, and is quick to seize any moving creature, be it insect, small fish, or crawfish. It would be well if the Grackle confined itself to the above diet. But it takes a heavy toll from the farmer's crops both spring and summer, its sturdy build and voracious appetite making it a serious menace. Not only does the Grackle despoil the farmer's crops but it is a disturber of the peace among other birds at nesting time. It rifles nests of eggs and callow young to such an extent as often to prevent other species making their homes in the vicinity of a colony of these birds. The nest is usually in trees or bushes near water, often in ornamental evergreens. The foundation and walls contain much mud. The eggs are bluish-white, spotted and scrawled with dark brown and black.

RUSTY BLACKBIRD   BREWER'S BLACKBIRD
FALL PLUMAGE   MALE   FEMALE
MALE, BREEDING ADULT

                                              FEMALE, RUSTY BLACKBIRD

COMMON GRACKLE
MALE   FEMALE

Scale about one-half

PLATE 77

COWBIRDS (Family *Icteridae*) AND STARLINGS (Family *Sturnidae*)

The cowbirds form a small group and are found only in the New World. They are all rather small, plain-colored birds. With a single exception, the Bay-winged Cowbird of Argentina, they are all parasitic, depositing their eggs in the nests of other birds and leaving them to be hatched and the young cared for by the foster-parents. Dr. Herbert Friedmann, who has studied this subject exhaustively, believes that they all originally nested normally, losing the nest-building instinct later.

The BROWN-HEADED COWBIRD, *Molothrus ater* (7-8.25), occurs from southern Canada south throughout the United States, and in most of Mexico; it winters in the southern United States and Mexico.

The Brown-headed Cowbird is the homeless hobo among North American birds, foisting its family upon the care of other birds usually smaller than itself. Whether it forms definite and enduring mating attachments is still something of a problem. Throughout the nesting season both sexes, joined later by the young, go roving about in flocks, the females detaching themselves for a brief period while depositing an egg in the nest of some hapless nearby bird. Some 200 species and subspecies have been listed as thus victimized, but commonly it is confined to a limited number of the smaller perching birds. Usually the eggs or young of the foster-bird are destroyed. The Cowbird may remove an egg from the nest before depositing her own. A few birds, notably the Yellow Warbler, bury the alien eggs, and, it may be, one or more of their own, by building a second nest over the first. This may be repeated several times, resulting in three- or four-storied nests. The eggs are white or bluish-white, more or less heavily marked with brown and gray.

The starlings are a numerous group of Old World birds, representatives of which have been introduced into various countries where they have thriven all too well. Besides the species that is now so well established in eastern North America a second, the Crested Mynah (*Aethiopsar cristatellus*), was introduced at Vancouver, B.C., and occasionally is found in Washington and Oregon.

The STARLING, *Sturnus vulgaris vulgaris* (7.50-8.50), was successfully introduced into New York City in 1890-91 after several previous failures. These birds, about a hundred in number, established themselves in Central Park and were the nucleus of the vast hordes that are now found throughout the eastern United States and Canada. About 1916 the Starling crossed the Alleghany Mountains and by 1936 was common and increasing in numbers as far west at least as the Mississippi River. By 1960 it had covered almost the entire North American continent, as had that other alien, the House Sparrow.

The adult male Starling, with its iridescent and mottled black dress and bright yellow bill, is a not unattractive bird. Its general food habits also are in its favor, and were it not for its habit of congregating and roosting in great numbers about buildings, together with its fondness for grain, berries, and the eggs and callow young of small birds, its presence might be regarded with less disfavor. But when all adverse conditions are considered, including its rapid increase and its usurpation of the rights of our native birds, the outlook is fraught with danger. It is another example of the lack of wisdom in introducing foreign animals or plants into new environments where the original controlling factors are absent.

STARLING

MALE, BREEDING ADULT   YOUNG MALE, FIRST WINTER

JUVENAL PLUMAGE

BROWN-HEADED COWBIRD

JUVENAL PLUMAGE

ADULT MALE   ADULT FEMALE

Scale about one-half

PLATE 78

TANAGERS (Family *Thraupidae*)

The tanagers are brilliantly colored birds found only in the New World. They are small birds, the majority averaging about six inches in length. About 220 species are known, confined mostly to the warmer, forested regions of Central and South America, only four species occurring as far north as the United States. The only tanager found as a summer resident in eastern Canada and the northern part of the eastern United States is the Scarlet Tanager. The Western Tanager, a largely yellow bird with black wings and a red face, nests in the Black Hills and occasionally wanders farther east. The Summer Tanager, entirely dull red, is a southeastern species that may stray into the Upper Midwest.

The SCARLET TANAGER, *Piranga olivacea* (6.50-7.50), breeds in southern Canada east from eastern Manitoba, south in the United States to Arkansas and the mountains of South Carolina; it winters in South America from Colombia to Peru.

The fully adult male Scarlet Tanager in the breeding season, with his gorgeous scarlet body and head and his jet black wings and tail, is a flash from the tropics transported to our northern woodlands. Perched in the open he glows like a brilliant flame. But when hidden away among the lights and shadows of the treetop leafage, gay as he is, he is by no means a conspicuous object, and were it not for his distinctive call note and burring song his presence would often be unsuspected. The Tanager is a forest-loving bird, commonly choosing open oak and elm woodlands, but among the evergreens farther north it is equally at home in the pines and spruces. The flimsy nest, through which the eggs may be seen from below, is commonly on a horizontal limb, out among the terminal branches and well up from the ground. The eggs are greenish-blue or greenish-white, marked with reddish-brown, chiefly at the larger end.

The Tanager's song is often compared with that of the Robin and the Rose-breasted Grosbeak, but although it is a strong, bright warble delivered leisurely, with a general resemblance to the songs of these birds, it is neither so full nor so sustained as their utterances. It has an undercurrent of harsh notes, giving it a double-toned quality, which can be imitated only by whistling and humming at the same time. This burred quality is also noticeable in its characteristic *chip-churr,* which is distinctly enunciated and unlike anything else heard in the northern woods.

The interesting sequence of plumages through which the male Tanager passes is well shown in the illustration. In the striped nestling plumage the sexes are alike. In the succeeding fall plumage the male is yellower and has browner wings and tail than the female. In this dress he goes to South America for the winter. While there he acquires a pale red body and a black tail, retaining the largely brown wings. In this garb he comes north, mates, and breeds. Following the nesting season a full molt occurs, after which the body is again yellowish-green and the entire wing becomes a clear black. Again he goes south, appearing much like the female, but both wings and tail are now black. Again in the south he acquires a red dress, this time a deeper scarlet, and returns north arrayed in full adult splendor. Twice a year thereafter the body color is changed—from scarlet to yellowish-green in the north, and from yellowish-green to scarlet in the south, each time passing through the dappled stage shown in the bird in the lower left-hand corner of the plate. The bright yellow bird in the left upper corner is in a freak plumage rarely seen among tanagers.

The food of the Scarlet Tanager is mainly animal matter—moths, even the larger species and including the gypsy and brown-tail; hairy caterpillars and other larvae, weevils, click- and leaf-beetles, flies, bugs, ants, and grasshoppers.

SCARLET TANAGER

ABNORMAL PLUMAGE	MALE, FULLY ADULT (BLACK WINGS)
(XANTHOCHROISM)	
MALE, WINTER	FEMALE
	JUVENAL PLUMAGE (NESTLING)
MALE, FIRST BREEDING PLUMAGE (BROWN WINGS)	
MOLTING MALE	

Scale about one-half

PLATE 79

GROSBEAKS, FINCHES, SPARROWS, AND BUNTINGS (Family *Fringillidae*)

This is the largest of all bird families, containing some 400 species, distributed throughout all parts of the world except Australia. The perching birds are the most highly developed of birds, and, as many authorities have accorded the sparrow tribe the topmost place in this group, they are thus at the very summit of the avian family tree. A great variety of common names are used for members of the sparrow family, such as finch, bunting, linnet, grosbeak, crossbill, longspur, junco, siskin, and sparrow. In many species the males are highly colored while the females are plain and dull-colored. Other species are inconspicuous, striped little birds, and the sexes are alike. Some of the finest and sweetest songsters belong to this family; other members have only weak, simple utterances or monotonous trills scarcely worthy the name of song. The typical sparrow bill is stout and cone-shaped, with the edges of the lower mandible rolled slightly inward and the base turned abruptly downward, forming a perfect instrument for cracking seeds, their principal food. Economically, the sparrow family is of greater value to man than any other group of birds. The food consists of from 65 to 75 per cent vegetable matter, chiefly weed and grass seeds, and 25 to 35 per cent insects, most of which are injurious species such as grasshoppers, cutworms, beetles, and caterpillars.

The CARDINAL, *Richmondena cardinalis* (7.50-9.25), occurs, in one or another of numerous subspecies, as a permanent resident throughout most of North America south of Canada, including Mexico. The Cardinal is one of several southern species that are extending their ranges northward. In recent years it has appeared and taken up its permanent residence in the northernmost of the United States, where it was previously unknown. It remains throughout the year where found. The Cardinal lives mostly in the undergrowth of open woodlands and in the shrubbery and tangled vines of parks and city yards. It is a frequent and much appreciated visitor to winter feeding stations. The nest is a loosely constructed affair placed in a bush or small tree at no great height from the ground. The eggs are white or pale bluish-white, marked with reddish-brown, chiefly at the larger end. The Cardinal may be a noisy bird, uttering a variety of notes, and both male and female are sweet singers. The song may be heard both winter and summer.

The ROSE-BREASTED GROSBEAK, *Pheucticus ludovicianus* (7-8.54), breeds in southern Canada east of the Rocky Mountains, south to the central and middle Atlantic states, and to Georgia in the mountains; it winters from southern Mexico to Colombia and Ecuador; it is accidental in migration in the Bahamas, West Indies, and the western United States. The song of the Rose-breasted Grosbeak is a loud, sweet, luscious warble, than which there is nothing more beautiful in the way of a warbled song in all the northern woodlands. The somewhat similar song of the Robin is heavier and more broken, and that of the Scarlet Tanager is marked and marred by occasional buzzing notes. The male Rose-breast assists in incubating the eggs and frequently sings while thus engaged. The female, too, sings short snatches of a sweet, warbled song, which she, like the male, may sing while sitting on the eggs or caring for the young. The nest is a flimsy affair placed not far from the ground in a tree or bush. The eggs are pale blue, spotted with brown. The usual food of the Rose-breast gives it high mark among the birds most useful to the farmer and horticulturist. It is one of the few birds that eat the potato-bug in large quantity. This trait has gained for it the name "Potato-bug Bird." Almost its only fault is a fondness for garden peas. When the supply is limited and unprotected, the Rose-breast and the Baltimore Oriole may leave but scanty picking for the rightful owner.

ROSE-BREASTED GROSBEAK

MALE, WINTER   FULLY ADULT BREEDING MALE (BLACK WINGS)
FEMALE

NESTLING, MALE   FIRST-YEAR BREEDING MALE (BROWN WINGS;
(JUVENAL PLUMAGE)   EXCEPTIONAL IN LACKING USUAL BLACK HEAD)

CARDINAL
FEMALE   MALE

Scale about one-half

PLATE 80

INDIGO BUNTING, PINE SISKIN, AND GOLDFINCH (Family *Fringillidae*)

The INDIGO BUNTING, *Passerina cyanea* (5.44-5.62), breeds in southern Canada east from Manitoba, and south in the United States to the Gulf states; it winters from southern Mexico to Panama, and in Cuba.

The pretty little male Indigo Bunting, arrayed nearly throughout in a brilliant blue, deeper in hue than the sky above, is an inhabitant with his plain-colored spouse of sparsely wooded brushy country, old clearings and windfalls grown up in second growth, and narrow strips of timber bordering lakes and streams. From an elevated perch he sings a sweet-toned but rather characterless ditty, delivered in a lazy fashion. He is an indefatigable performer, beginning with the dawn and ending only when the Whip-poor-will begins his evening plaint. All through the hot months of summer he continues his *swee-swee-swee, sweet-sweet-sweet,* after most birds are silent. The nest of grasses, weed stalks, and rootlets is placed near the ground in bushes. The eggs are pale bluish-white, unmarked. The Indigo Bunting is a frequent victim of the Cowbird.

The AMERICAN GOLDFINCH, *Spinus tristis* (4.50-5), as a species breeds throughout most of the United States from southern Canada southward. In winter it is found over most of the United States range, south to Vera Cruz.

If the actions and expressions of birds are any indication of their dispositions and feelings, the handsome little Goldfinch is surely one of the most joyous and lighthearted of all our feathered throng. Sociable and genial among its kind, cheery and musical of voice, and gay and happy in demeanor, it goes frolicking through the summer time in little troops or couplets, with an abandon and a happy-go-lucky air that suggest never care or a duty the whole year round. While its neighbors are occupied with the many exactions of family affairs or are subdued by the trials and limitations of the molting season, the Goldfinch makes the long summer days sweet with its blithesome notes and its ever sprightly and jolly ways. Even after assuming the cares of raising a family as the summer wanes, its spirits seem never dampened. The neat little nest of grasses, plant-down, and thistle-pappus is built in an upright crotch in a bush, sapling, or tree. The eggs are pale bluish-white, unmarked.

The PINE SISKIN, *Spinus pinus* (4.50-5.25), breeds chiefly in the coniferous forests of Alaska, southern Canada, the northern United States, and south in the higher mountain ranges as far as southern Mexico; it winters over much of this area.

The little Pine Siskin, like the crossbills and the Evening Grosbeak, is possessed of a gypsy-like wanderlust that takes it now here, now there, and only irregularly and seemingly by chance back again to the same locality. Thus it goes wandering through the land, few or many together, winter and summer, settling for a season and rearing its family in most unexpected places. Normally it belongs in the coniferous forests of the north, but it has been found nesting among cultivated evergreens far from such surroundings. In some respects the Siskin is like its near relative, the Goldfinch, and in others like the crossbills. It resembles the latter in its indifference to any established breeding territory, in certain of its feeding habits, and in its tame and familiar ways. Like the Goldfinch it is sprightly and quick in its movements, and its ordinary notes and incessant twittering suggest the voice of that bird, though the Siskin's voice has an added creaky quality that is distinctive. The nest is in an evergreen tree, and the eggs are pale bluish-white, sparsely marked with reddish-brown.

INDIGO BUNTING

PINE SISKIN

MALE, BREEDING ADULT

FEMALE, BREEDING ADULT

MOLTING MALE

AMERICAN GOLDFINCH

WINTER

MALE, BREEDING ADULT

FEMALE, BREEDING ADULT

Scale about one-half

PLATE 81

PURPLE FINCH, REDPOLLS, AND PINE GROSBEAK (Family *Fringillidae*)

The PURPLE FINCH, *Carpodacus purpureus* (5.84-6.25), as a species breeds in the evergreen forests of Canada and the northern United States and farther south in the mountains; it winters from the southern part of its breeding range to the Gulf coast and Lower California. The Purple Finch is a common winter visitor at feeding stations where it avidly feeds on small seeds. The voice of the Purple Finch is loud, rich, and liquid, and both the brightly colored males and the second-year males in the plumage of the female utter a prolonged and varied warble that is replete with real melody and that bursts forth and flows on rapturously as though from a soul full of joy. On the breeding ground the rambling, early spring song is replaced by a more definite, assertive effort—the so-called "territory" song—which is, however, equally musical and pleasing and of the same warbling type. It is one of the choicest bird songs of the northern spruce and cedar swamps where the Purple Finch spends its summers. The performer sometimes indulges in a flight song. The nest is usually in evergreens, rarely in deciduous trees or bushes; the eggs are blue, marked with brown, chiefly about the larger end.

The COMMON REDPOLL, *Acanthis flammea* (5.11-5.50), makes its summer home in the far north of both hemispheres and wanders south into temperate latitudes in the winter. Individuals of several races may be associated in the same winter flocks. The cheery, fluffy, pretty little Redpoll leaves its summer home in arctic America with the first advent of autumn, and retreating southward before the deepening snows and failing food supply, reaches the northern United States in little straggling companies as early as the first half of October. It is often found feeding in open weedy fields even in the severest weather. Toward spring the flocks coalesce and then often number many thousands. Sometimes this bird fails to appear in such numbers and then again there are "Redpoll years" when it is abundant. Toward spring the Redpoll utters a clear and rapid *tre-re-re-re* which is no doubt a prelude to a more musical performance on the nesting ground in the far north.

The HOARY REDPOLL, *Acanthis hornemanni* (5-5.69), breeds in boreal North America and northeastern Siberia, and comes south into the United States and to Japan in winter. The Hoary Redpoll, as its name implies, is a light-colored bird—usually light enough to be readily distinguished among its darker companions. In voice and habits it is identical with the other redpolls.

The PINE GROSBEAK, *Pinicola enucleator* (9-10), as a species breeds in the northern forests of Europe and North America and in Kamchatka and wanders south in the winter into temperate latitudes. The Pine Grosbeak is a large, bold-looking bird of a tame and unsuspicious nature. The handsome rose-red old males form a pleasing contrast with the much more numerous somber-colored members of the winter flocks. The usual call note is a loud but mellow and sweet whistle, and occasionally there may be heard snatches of a low, pleasing song, which is said to develop in the springtime into a sustained, rich, melodious warble somewhat like that of the Purple Finch. The Pine Grosbeak's attachment to evergreen forests is shown by the fact that wherever it goes in its wanderings it is ever on the outlook for groves of pines and spruces, cultivated or native. The Pine Grosbeak often feeds on weeds and low bushes searching for seeds and berries.

PURPLE FINCH   HOARY REDPOLL
  FEMALE
      MALE

            COMMON REDPOLL
        FEMALE   MALE

        PINE GROSBEAK
                  FEMALE AND IMMATURE
    MALE

          Scale about one-half

PLATE 82

THE CROSSBILLS AND THE EVENING GROSBEAK (Family *Fringillidae*)

The RED CROSSBILL, *Loxia curvirostra* (5.50-6.25), is almost cosmopolitan in its distribution in the evergreen forests of the Northern Hemisphere. It is well known for being the most erratic wanderer among birds. Vast invasions may occur with some even reaching the Arizona deserts or the plains of Texas, whereas the next year they may be hard to find even in the northern forests. Thinking of crossbills brings to one's mind a picture of the tapering spruce spires of the northern woodlands. A group of busy little birds in varied plumage, clinging to the cones and with their crossed scissor-like bills prying open the cones enabling the tongues to nimbly extract the hidden seeds, completes the picture. Satisfied, they are off together in waving, zigzag flight, uttering as they go a rapid chatter interspersed with a sharp, metallic call. During the nesting season they have a sweet, warbling song. The nest is a deep, well-built structure, usually on a horizontal limb of an evergreen tree, well out from the trunk. The eggs are bluish- or greenish-white, spotted and penciled with shades of brown and lavender, chiefly at the larger end.

The WHITE-WINGED CROSSBILL, *Loxia leucoptera* (6-6.50), breeds in Alaska and throughout Canada, and in the evergreen forests of the northern United States east from Minnesota; also in the mountains of New York and New Hampshire. It winters in much of its breeding range and wanders south in the United States as far as Kansas and North Carolina. This Crossbill also displays freakish and erratic habits. It shows but little attachment to any particular region, nesting in one place one year and in another the next. While still associated in flocks they mate and begin nesting in late January and February, even though the weather is still bitter cold and the ground deeply covered with snow. The nesting period is prolonged throughout the spring and even at times until late in the summer. The song of the White-winged is said to be superior to that of the Red Crossbill, delivered, it may be, from a topmost perch or as a gushing, ecstatic flight song consisting of sweet warbled notes and canary-like trills. The nest resembles that of the Red Crossbill. The eggs are pale blue, marked with black and lilac, chiefly at the larger end.

The EVENING GROSBEAK, *Hesperiphona vespertina* (7.50-8.25), breeds in central and western Canada, in the northern United States, and in the western mountains south as far as southern Mexico; it winters from its breeding range irregularly southward. For the eastern race an east and west movement of over 1200 miles has been shown from banding operations (New Hampshire on the east, western Minnesota on the west). In the full perfection of its nuptial dress the Evening Grosbeak is a bird of singular and striking beauty. With its unheralded appearance among the dwellings of man and its tame and fearless demeanor, it rarely fails to attract and hold the attention of even the casual observer. It usually nests in the spruce and pine forests of the north, wandering south in the winter where groves of box elder and hackberry attract it, for it is especially fond of the fruit of these trees. The nest is a loosely built affair, resting far out on a horizontal limb. The eggs are greenish-blue or pale bluish-green, marked with shades of brown, chiefly at the larger end. The Evening Grosbeak has been found in two or three instances nesting in deciduous trees within the confines of a Manitoban town. The usual call notes are a loud piping whistle and a lower, beaded utterance resembling the notes of the waxwings. As spring approaches the notes acquire a more mellow character, and the united voices of a flock performing in unison is not unattractive, though not particularly musical. It has been likened to a spring hyla-chorus.

WHITE-WINGED CROSSBILL   RED CROSSBILL
JUVENAL PLUMAGE   ADULT FEMALE
ADULT FEMALE   ADULT MALE
ADULT MALE   JUVENAL PLUMAGE
EVENING GROSBEAK
MALE, JUVENAL PLUMAGE
ADULT MALE
ADULT FEMALE

Scale about one-half

PLATE 83

SPARROWS (Family *Fringillidae*)

The SAVANNAH SPARROW, *Passerculus sandwichensis* (5.25-6), breeds throughout North America, and southward into Guatemala. It winters from southern United States into Central America and Mexico. The song of the Savannah Sparrow is a brief musical trill, high-pitched and thin in quality and with little carrying power—*tsip-tsip-tsip se-e-e-sr-r-r*. The eggs are grayish-white, marked with reddish-brown.

The SHARP-TAILED SPARROW, *Ammospiza caudacuta* (4.50-5), is largely confined to the salt marshes of the Atlantic coast, but a wide-ranging inland population formerly called Nelson's Sparrow nests in sloughs and prairie marshes. It breeds in the wet marshes of central Canada and adjacent parts of the United States and winters in the South Atlantic and Gulf states. The Sharp-tailed and Leconte's sparrows are very similar in habits. They may be found together, in wet boggy marshes where the water is ankle- or knee-deep. Both have brief, buzzing songs, little more than a wheezy gasp, that of the Sharp-tail being the more insignificant. Few nests have been found. The eggs are bluish-green, marked with light brown and purplish, chiefly around the larger end.

The GRASSHOPPER SPARROW, *Ammodramus savannarum* (5-5.25), breeds over most of the United States, locally in southern Canada and the Greater Antilles, and winters south to Central America. The Grasshopper Sparrow is a bird of grassy upland fields and prairies. The usual song is an insect-like buzz, so weak that it carries but a very short distance. A brief flight song is more musical. The eggs are white, marked with reddish-brown, chiefly around the larger end.

HENSLOW'S SPARROW, *Passerherbulus henslowii* (4.90-5.25), breeds in Ontario and in the United States east of the Great Plains, and winters in the southern United States. Henslow's Sparrow is a tiny mite of a bird, lost for the most part in the dense growth of the marshes and adjacent uplands that it loves so well. Its presence may be revealed to a keen and attentive ear by the briefest and weakest of all bird songs, a mere *tsee-wick* or *shl-pp*. An occasional flight song is more pretentious. The eggs are white, marked with reddish-brown.

BAIRD'S SPARROW, *Ammodramus bairdii* (5.30-5.60), breeds on the prairies of south central Canada and in the United States from Montana to western Minnesota; it winters from central Texas to northern Mexico. Baird's Sparrow is a bird of the western plains. It so closely resembles the Savannah Sparrow in appearance and habits that it is not easy to distinguish the two in the field. The songs, however, are different enough to be recognizable after close study. Baird's song is more of a tinkling warble than the weak trill of the Savannah. The eggs are dull white, marked and lined with brown, forming a wreath around the larger end.

LECONTE'S SPARROW, *Passerherbulus caudacutus* (4.50-5.25), breeds in the meadows and marshes of central Canada and south to North Dakota and Minnesota; it winters in the south central United States and the Gulf and South Atlantic states. Leconte's Sparrow, clothed in golden hue, is one of the prettiest of the smaller sparrows, but it clings so closely to the dense cover of the bogs in which it dwells that its acquaintance is difficult to make. With upturned head and strenuous effort the male delivers a brief, gasping wheeze, which is the usual song. The eggs vary from grayish-white to greenish-blue, marked and lined more or less heavily with brown.

SAVANNAH SPARROW   GRASSHOPPER SPARROW

SHARP-TAILED SPARROW   HENSLOW'S SPARROW

ADULT

JUVENAL PLUMAGE   BAIRD'S SPARROW

LECONTE'S SPARROW

ADULT   JUVENAL PLUMAGE

Scale about one-half

PLATE 84

SPARROWS AND BUNTINGS (Family *Fringillidae*)

The birds grouped in this plate all live on plains, in open fields, or in sparse woodlands, and all nest on the ground. Otherwise they have nothing in common except that they all belong to the sparrow family.

The VESPER SPARROW, *Pooecetes gramineus* (6-6.50), in one or another of three subspecies breeds throughout southern Canada and south in the western United States to the Mexican border and to just north of the Gulf states in the eastern United States. It winters from the southern United States to southern Mexico. The plain little Vesper Sparrow is a common roadside bird in open places, wild or cultivated. Old roads best suit its fancy, where, like the Horned Lark, it can take dust-baths. The song is a humble but sweet effort of several low notes followed by simple trills. It is by no means a "vesper" song but may be heard throughout the day. The old names, "Grass Finch" and "Bay-winged Bunting," are more appropriate than the present name. The eggs are dull white, marked with brown, heaviest at the larger end.

The LARK BUNTING, *Calamospiza melanocorys* (6.50-7.50), breeds on the central plains of North America and winters from southern Texas and Arizona south to central Mexico; it is accidental in migration in both the east and west coast states. The Lark Bunting is essentially a bird of the high, rolling, treeless plains. It avoids the lowlands and finds congenial surroundings on bare, boulder-strewn bluffs. In general appearance and habits it is the Bobolink of the dry, upland prairie. The "White-winged Blackbird," as the Lark Bunting was formerly called, is an accomplished songster. On the western plains, where it abounds, it is one of the most attractive of the prairie birds. The song is delivered for the most part while the bird is poised in the air, and consists of a series of trills uttered rapidly in a full rich tone, not unlike the singing of a fine canary. The nest is well concealed under tufts of grass or weeds and the eggs are pale blue, unmarked.

The DICKCISSEL, or BLACK-THROATED BUNTING, *Spiza americana* (6.12-6.75), breeds in southern Canada east from Manitoba and in the United States east from Wyoming and south to the Gulf states, and winters from southern Central America to Colombia, Venezuela, and Trinidad. It is now rare east of the Alleghanies. The Dickcissel is a gypsy among the birds, here one year and somewhere else the next. There are "Dickcissel years" and years when the bird is almost entirely absent. It should be looked for in clover fields, alfalfa fields, or upland grasslands. The song is simple and jingling, beginning with a *dick, dick* and ending with a *cissel-cissel-cissel*. The nest may be in a bush but is usually well concealed on the ground; the eggs are pale blue, unmarked.

The LARK SPARROW, *Chondestes grammacus* (6.40-6.92), breeds from about the Canadian International Boundary south throughout the United States west of the Alleghanies; it winters in the Gulf states and eastern Mexico, and from northern California to Guatemala. The Lark Sparrow will be found on close inspection to be a handsome little bird, and it is possessed also of even greater charms. The male is a musician of exceptional ability. His song is long and varied, a series of runs and trills, liquid and clear, poured forth with great fervor and animation. He is an ardent wooer, strutting about with feathers puffed out, wings drooping, and tail expanded—like a little turkey cock. Let a rival or rivals appear and there ensues immediately a fierce and noisy combat. The nest is a deep cup, well hidden, and the eggs are white, spotted and scrawled with dark brown and black.

VESPER SPARROW   LARK BUNTING
                                    MALE, BREEDING ADULT

DICKCISSEL   FEMALE
       FEMALE
   MALE   LARK SPARROW
                                             ADULT
                                   JUVENAL PLUMAGE

Scale about one-half

PLATE 85

JUNCO (Family *Fringillidae*) AND ENGLISH SPARROW (Family *Ploceidae*)

The SLATE-COLORED JUNCO, *Junco hyemalis* (5.75-6.25), breeds in the coniferous forests of Alaska, Canada, and the northern United States, and in the Alleghany Mountains to northern Georgia. It winters from the southern part of its breeding range to the Gulf coast.

Juncos wintering in the north seek the shelter of brush-grown and weedy places, especially deep ravines. There they bear temperatures of many degrees below zero, seemingly without discomfort as long as the supply of grass and weed seeds holds out. Deep snows may drive them elsewhere and they become regular visitors to feeding stations, where they prefer to feed on the ground rather than at an elevated counter, though in time they may follow the lead of the chickadees and nuthatches. Like their companions, the Tree Sparrows, they have at this time both a "whisper song" and a loud, sweet warble, and in the early spring a much more pretentious effort very different from the simple, Chippy-like trill commonly heard on the nesting grounds. The nest is on the ground, well concealed, and the eggs are white or bluish-white, marked with reddish-brown, sometimes forming a wreath about the larger end.

The OREGON JUNCO, *Junco oreganus* (5.75-6.25, not illustrated), with a black hood contrasting with its lighter brownish sides and with a brownish back, is an occasional winter visitor from the western mountains.

The HOUSE or ENGLISH SPARROW, *Passer domesticus* (5.75-6.25), was first introduced into North America in 1850 from the Old World, where it ranges over a vast area. It is a permanent resident. It is well established throughout the whole of North America.

Following the importation of eight pairs into Brooklyn in the fall of 1850, by directors of the Brooklyn Institute, numerous introductions and transplantings of small and large groups of these readily adaptable birds took place until it had been planted and fostered in over a hundred cities throughout the United States and Canada. For a time there was great enthusiasm over the venture, no one seeming to realize the disastrous consequences that were to follow. The motives that prompted its introduction were partly pure sentiment on the part of European residents in foreign countries and partly the mistaken idea that it would be more valuable than the native birds as a destroyer of the caterpillars and other insects infesting city shade trees. The food of the House Sparrow consists chiefly of grain, berries, fruit, and garden vegetables. Comparatively few insects are eaten and of these a large proportion is made up of useful species. It may at times destroy large numbers of caterpillars infesting shade trees and garden crops, especially cabbages, but on the whole it is an undesirable and harmful bird, not only doing comparatively little good itself but driving away and taking the rightful place of native birds of much greater value. Its habit of nesting and roosting in great numbers in ornamental vines on buildings, and the consequent defacement that results, makes it a nuisance. It can never be entirely eradicated, but in small places the numbers can be kept down by systematic and repeated destruction of the nests and shooting of the birds.

The male House Sparrow is an ardent wooer. Everyone must be familiar with its jaunty appearance as it does a hopping dance with trailing wings around the indifferent object of its attention. It has a few mellow, warbled notes in the spring, which may be regarded as a song. It nests from early spring until fall, raising several numerous broods. The eggs are white or brownish-white, speckled with shades of brown.

SLATE-COLORED JUNCO   ENGLISH SPARROW
MALE, BREEDING ADULT   MALE
IMMATURE, FALL   FEMALE
FEMALE, BREEDING ADULT

JUVENAL PLUMAGE

Scale about one-half

PLATE 86

SPARROWS (Family *Fringillidae*)

This is another group of the small striped sparrows that make a considerable part of the sparrow family difficult for the beginner in bird study. The question of identity is rendered even more complex by the fact that the old and young differ greatly in plumage.

The TREE SPARROW, *Spizella arborea* (6-6.60), breeds in the far north and winters in Ontario and the United States, south nearly to the Gulf states and the Mexican boundary. In early spring the Tree Sparrow passes northward from the United States to its summer home in boreal regions, and returns in the late fall in augmented numbers to spend the winter in weed-grown fields and bottomlands. It is a cheery fellow with a sweet voice and sings all through the fall, winter, and spring. Wintering Tree Sparrows and Juncos love the same kind of places and are often found together until the nesting urge sends them on their way and breaks up the companionship. The nest is on or near the ground among the spruces or on the tundra of northern Canada; the eggs are greenish-blue or pale greenish, with reddish-brown markings.

The CHIPPING SPARROW, *Spizella passerina* (5-5.85), breeds over most of North America, and winters in the southern part of its breeding range to northern Mexico. The little Chipping Sparrow, "Chippy," or "Hair-bird," is the most thoroughly domesticated of all our native sparrows. It dwells familiarly about our homes and builds its nest in the ornamental shrubbery, even in the vines and shrubs about our doorsteps. Long horsehairs, when obtainable, enter largely into the lining of the little grass nest, three or four feet from the ground and preferably in a small evergreen. The eggs are greenish-blue, marked with brown, chiefly at the larger end. The song of the Chippy is a simple, unmusical repetition of the same note, uttered rapidly in a monotone—*chip, chip, chip, chip*—sometimes run together to form an almost unbroken trill.

The FIELD SPARROW, *Spizella pusilla* (5.10-6), breeds in the United States east of the Rocky Mountains, and winters in the southern United States and northeastern Mexico. The Field Sparrow is a southern species that has been extending its range northward in recent years. Its preference is for bushy hillsides, abandoned fields, and open woods. Its plain dress is compensated for by a sweetly plaintive, appealing voice, which finds expression in a song beginning with four or five distinct, clearly whistled notes and ending in a rapid, pleasing trill with a slightly rising inflection. The nest is on or near the ground, and the eggs are pale greenish-blue, bluish-white, or white, spotted with brown, chiefly at the larger end.

The CLAY-COLORED SPARROW, *Spizella pallida* (5-5.50), breeds in the interior of North America from southern Canada south as far as Colorado and Illinois; it winters from the south central United States to southern Mexico and is casual farther west and in the eastern states. The light-colored, plainly garbed, inconspicuous little Clay-colored Sparrow is an inhabitant of brushland and small tree-growth, and might easily be overlooked were it not for its incessant and characteristic "song"—a thin, unmusical, cicada-like, buzzing *ze, ze, ze, ze, ze, ze*. On close inspection the head markings with the clay-colored patch back of the eye will be found distinctive. The nestling is so like the nestling Chippy that it is difficult to distinguish them. The rather loosely built nest of grass and twigs is near the ground in a bush or an evergreen, rarely on the ground in a tussock of grass; the eggs are greenish-blue, marked with brown, chiefly around the larger end.

TREE SPARROW, ADULT

CHIPPING SPARROW   FIELD SPARROW
ADULT   ADULT
JUVENAL PLUMAGE   JUVENAL PLUMAGE

CLAY-COLORED SPARROW
ADULT   JUVENAL PLUMAGE

Scale about one-half

PLATE 87

HARRIS', THE WHITE-CROWNED, AND WHITE-THROATED SPARROWS
(Family *Fringillidae*)

The handsome head ornaments of the adults of this group of sparrows set them off and distinguish them from the more somber-hued of their ground-loving associates. But the young birds that flood the hedgerows and weed patches in the fall are plainly colored and striped as are those of so many other species of the sparrow family.

HARRIS' SPARROW, *Zonotrichia querula* (7.20-7.94), breeds in north central Canada from Hudson Bay to Great Bear Lake, and winters in the Great Basin, and the southern Great Plains east to the Mississippi River. In the migration season in the interior United States the bird lover, loitering beside a vine-tangled hedgerow or exploring the possibilities of a pile of brush in a recent clearing, may, in late spring or mid-fall, startle into view a large, handsome, black-hooded red-billed bird—the Harris' Sparrow. It may utter a fairly loud *chink* or *clink* and possibly, in a quavering plaintive voice, a subdued, warbling song, which, at nesting time in the far north, develops into a more definite, striking song with something of the quality of the White-throat but with a warbling termination. The nest has been rarely found until recently. It is on the ground, and the eggs are pale blue-green, marked with brown.

The WHITE-CROWNED SPARROW, *Zonotrichia leucophrys,* is a bird of the edges of cool evergreen forests from northern Alaska across Canada to Labrador, south in the western mountains to Arizona, but in the east only to southeastern Quebec. The species winters through much of central and southern United States, Mexico, and Cuba.

Two well-marked populations are found in the Upper Midwest, one with the white line over the eye extending to the base of the bill so that the region in front of the eyes is white was previously called "Gambel's Sparrow" (*Z. l. gambelii*). The other, which has the white line ending at the eye, has been called the White-crowned Sparrow (*Z. l. leucophrys*). "Gambel's Sparrow" is a distinctive population of the White-crowned species, and may sometimes be noticed in the field.

White-crowned Sparrows sing not infrequently during migration, especially in late spring. On its nesting ground its song, similar in quality to the White-throats, begins with clear, whistled notes and ends with notes in a husky or whispered whistle. The nest is on the ground or in a low bush, and the eggs are bluish-white to greenish-white, thickly marked with brown and sometimes black.

The WHITE-THROATED SPARROW, *Zonotrichia albicollis* (6.50-7.45), breeds in the coniferous forests of Canada east from Mackenzie, and in the northern United States from Montana to New England, south in the Alleghany Mountains to northern Pennsylvania; it winters chiefly in the United States from Massachusetts and the Ohio Valley south to Florida and northeastern Mexico. There is no more welcome and pleasing sound in the spring than the clear, whistled song of the White-throated Sparrow, which is one of the few migrants that sing freely as they pass northward. The song begins with two or three deliberate notes of varying pitch, followed by a quavering trill. Amid the comparative silence of the northern pines, where the White-throat makes its home, its sweet plaintive cadence rarely fails to attract attention. The nest is on the ground or in a low bush, and the eggs are bluish-white, marked with pale reddish-brown.

HARRIS' SPARROW
YOUNG, FIRST FALL   ADULT

WHITE-CROWNED SPARROW
ADULT
                                                    GAMBEL'S SPARROW, ADULT
YOUNG IN FALL

WHITE-THROATED SPARROW
JUVENAL PLUMAGE   ADULT

Scale about one-half

PLATE 88

TOWHEE AND SPARROWS (Family *Fringillidae*)

Grouped about the two central figures in the plate, a pair of towhees, are several more of the plain-colored, striped sparrows that puzzle the tyro in the field until the peculiar mannerisms and voice of each have been stored in the memory.

The FOX SPARROW, *Passerella iliaca* (6.50-7.38), in its numerous subspecies occurs throughout North America, breeding in the boreal evergreen forests of Alaska and Canada and south in the high mountains of the western United States; it winters in the southern United States and in northern Lower California. The handsome Fox Sparrow is a shy inhabitant of the undergrowth and is an expert "scratcher," making the dry leaves fly in its search for hidden seeds and insects. It is a sweet singer, the song consisting of clear, musical whistles, rich and pure in quality. The nest is on or near the ground, and the eggs are greenish, marked with dull reddish-brown.

The SONG SPARROW, *Melospiza melodia* (5.75-6.75), occurs throughout nearly all North America, northwestern Mexico, and on outlying islands. So physically variable is this bird in relation to the varied environments in which it nests that over thirty subspecies are recognized. The more northern breeding birds retreat southward in the winter. Although the Song Sparrow prefers lowlands, its cheery lay may be heard amidst widely varying surroundings. The song varies endlessly but consists commonly of a few introductory notes, followed by a sweet, musical trill. The nest is usually on the ground but may be raised a foot or so. The eggs are white or greenish-white, heavily marked with brown.

The RUFOUS-SIDED TOWHEE, *Pipilo erythrophthalmus,* nests from southern Canada throughout most of the United States south through Mexico to Guatemala. It varies much from region to region; those in Florida have white eyes, those in the western mountains have white-striped backs, and those in Mexico have green backs. Wherever it occurs, it has rufous sides and similar habits. It skulks in the brush, scratching for food in the leaf litter. The male is most frequently seen as he perches on an elevated branch and gives his call note of *Che-wink* (another of the common names) or his simple but forceful song *chipper-che-e-e.* The first two syllables are sharp and distinct, the latter part a trill. The nest is commonly on or near the ground. The eggs are white or pinkish white, marked with reddish-brown.

The LINCOLN'S SPARROW, *Melospiza lincolnii* (5.62-6), breeds in the coniferous forests of Canada and the northern United States, south in the mountains to southern California and New Mexico; it winters from southern United States to northern Central America. In migration Lincoln's Sparrow is a shy, secretive denizen of the thick undergrowth and dense weed patches. In appearance it resembles a delicately marked Song Sparrow, with a buffy breastband and without the dark central breast spot. On its northern nesting grounds it is said to have a varied and musical but rather weak song. The nest is on the ground, and the eggs resemble the Song Sparrow's.

The SWAMP SPARROW, *Melospiza georgiana* (5.12-5.88), is a bird of eastern North America, breeding from southern Mackenzie south to North Dakota and the middle Atlantic states; it winters from the southern part of its breeding range to middle Mexico. The simple but rather musical trill of the Swamp Sparrow comes from the tangled growth of the wet marshes and sloughs where it lives. Occasionally the bird rises in the air and delivers a much more pretentious flight song. The nest is concealed in a tuft of coarse grass. The eggs are bluish-white, heavily marked with reddish-brown and blackish.

FOX SPARROW   SONG SPARROW

RUFOUS-SIDED TOWHEE
MALE   FEMALE

LINCOLN'S SPARROW

SWAMP SPARROW

JUVENAL PLUMAGE   ADULT

Scale about one-half

PLATE 89

LONGSPURS (Family *Fringillidae*), HORNED LARK (Family *Alaudidae*), AND PIPITS (Family *Motacillidae*)

Birds of three families are assembled in this illustration chiefly for the purpose of direct comparison. They are all eminently ground birds and, where they occur together, may be easily confused by the beginner in bird study. The longspurs hop while the others walk, and the pipits dip or wag the tail with each step, which serves to distinguish them from the Horned Lark and the Vesper Sparrow, both of which have about the same amount of white in the tail as the pipits. Horned Larks are not always as strikingly colored as those in the plate, which adds to the confusion. If the little tufts of feathers on the head can be seen they are a safe guide. All the birds here shown have sweet, musical voices. The song is delivered while the birds are circling high in the air. The longspurs flutter back to earth like a falling leaf, but the larks and pipits return by a precipitate, vertical dive, so rapid as to be difficult to follow with the eye.

McCown's Longspur, *Rhynchophanes mccownii* (5.75-6), breeds on the Great Plains of interior North America, and winters from the south central United States to northwestern Mexico. The nesting ranges of this and the next species have been reduced materially by the breaking up and cultivation of the virgin prairie, which seems to be essential to normal homemaking. The nest is on the ground, and the eggs are dull white or buffy, marked and lined with dark brown and black.

The Chestnut-collared Longspur, *Calcarius ornatus* (5.75-6.40), breeds on the prairies of interior North America, and winters from the south central United States to the high plateaus of southern Mexico. Fluttering overhead like big butterflies and filling the air with a bubbling melody pleasing to the ear, the many little Chestnut-collared or Black-bellied Longspurs are an attractive feature of the high, rolling, wild prairies of the interior of North America. The nest is usually amid short scanty grass, and the eggs are dull greenish-white or drab, marked with brown and lavender.

The Horned Lark, *Eremophila alpestris* (6.62-8), occurs as a species over much of the Old and New Worlds. This species varies greatly in color intensity in different regions, especially in the amounts of yellow on the head. The Horned Lark, or Shore Lark, is a common roadside bird, especially along old dusty roads, for it is a confirmed and vigorous duster. The spring flight song of the male, coming from high in the air and ending with the plunge to earth, is a spectacular performance. The nest is on the ground, built with little or no attempt at concealment, and the eggs are dull glossy white, thickly marked with pale brown and lavender. It is the earliest of our small birds to nest.

Sprague's Pipit, *Anthus spragueii* (6.25-7), breeds on the interior plains of North America, and winters from the Gulf region south to southern Mexico. Sprague's Pipit is the "Skylark" of the western prairies. The male, in the nesting season, spends much of his time high in the air, almost invisible except against a fleecy cloud. The sweet tinkling song, floating down to earth, announces his presence. The nest is concealed in dense grass, usually arched over; the eggs are dull white, faintly marked with light brown and lilac.

The Water or American Pipit, *Anthus spinoletta* (6-7), occurs in both the Old and the New Worlds. It breeds under arctic and alpine conditions; it winters from northern California and the middle eastern states south to the Gulf coast and Guatemala. In the early spring and late fall there may be seen almost anywhere in the United States a slender, plain-colored little bird, walking daintily along the water's edge or on plowed or barren fields, accompanying each step with a gentle wagging of the tail. This is the Water Pipit on its way to or from its summer home on the tundras.

PLATE 89

BIRD PORTRAITS IN COLOR

Walter Alois Weber - 1930

McCOWN'S LONGSPUR
FEMALE   MALE, BREEDING ADULT

HORNED LARK
FEMALE
MALE

CHESTNUT-COLLARED LONGSPUR
FEMALE   MALE, BREEDING ADULT

JUVENAL PLUMAGE

SPRAGUE'S PIPIT

WATER PIPIT

Scale about one-half

PLATE 90

LONGSPURS AND SNOW BUNTING (Family *Fringillidae*)

The LAPLAND LONGSPUR, *Calcarius lapponicus* (6.25-6.90), breeds on the arctic tundras in both the Old and the New Worlds, and in winter migrates south to more temperate climes. In North America it may reach the middle states and Texas, rarely Kentucky and South Carolina. It was this Longspur in Alaska that so appealed to the fancy of John Burroughs, on his memorable trip to that faraway country, that he called it the "Northland Bobolink" and composed an attractive poem about it, which closes with the words,

> At morn, at noon, in pallid light,
> We heard thy song and saw thy flight,
> While I, sighing, could but think
> Of my boyhood's Bobolink.

In their semiannual migrations to and fro the Lapland Longspurs pass both by day and by night at no great height above the prairie in vast straggling flocks, all the birds chirping and whistling as they go. But when established at a feeding place the birds take the air in dense, noisy flocks, circling and dipping in intricate evolutions until ready to alight again.

SMITH'S LONGSPUR, *Calcarius pictus* (5.70-6.50), breeds on the barren grounds of arctic North America from Mackenzie east to Hudson Bay, and winters in the southern United States from Kansas to Texas; it goes east in migration to the prairies of Illinois and Indiana. Smith's Longspur or the "Painted Longspur," an apt name formerly much used, very closely resembles the Lapland in general habits. Breeding in the far north, it migrates, spring and fall, over the open plains, stopping to feed in weed-grown cornfields and similar places. It is frequently in company with the Lapland.

The SNOW BUNTING, *Plectrophenax nivalis* (6.40-7.12), breeds in the arctic and sub-arctic regions of both North America and Europe; in North America it migrates south-ward in winter into the northern United States, irregularly as far as the central states and rarely to South Carolina and Florida; in Europe, to the Mediterranean, north Africa, the Canary Islands, and the Azores. The Snow Bunting, in its southward fall flight, enters the United States in early fall, and, if it is to be a "Snow Bunting year," the first few arrivals are soon followed by large flocks, which, when the snow is deep in the northern states, pass on southward where the weed seeds, on which it feeds so largely, are more easily obtained. On the return spring flight the close flock-formation is usually not so evident. The birds are distributed widely over a vast front, passing steadily onward both day and night, often for many hours at a time. While sojourning in the south the Snow Bunting, or "Snow-flake," is a ground-loving bird, seldom alighting in trees, and roosting at night on the earth or in the snow beneath the shelter of some tuft of grass or clod of earth. It is at such times gregarious in the highest degree, and the vast flocks that frequently assemble toward spring may almost obscure the skies as they tower above the weed fields from which they arise, whirling and circling in perfect unison, now up, now down, making with their thousands of wings a noise like the rushing of the wind. This wing music is accompanied by an unbroken chorus of chirps and purring sounds from the countless tiny throats. With the sun shining brightly, it is a charming sight to see a flock of these beautiful white birds—for at a little distance they seem nearly pure white—disporting themselves in graceful evo-lutions, appearing like a drifting cloud of eddying snowflakes, from which they take their most appropriate name.

PLATE 90

SMITH'S LONGSPUR

MALE, BREEDING ADULT   FEMALE

MALE, WINTER

LAPLAND LONGSPUR

FEMALE, WINTER

MALE, WINTER

MALE, BREEDING ADULT

SNOW BUNTING

MALE, NEARLY FULL BREEDING PLUMAGE

FEMALE, WINTER

Scale about one-half

INDEX

INDEX

INDEX

INDEX

INDEX

INDEX

INDEX

INDEX

INDEX

INDEX

NOTES

NOTES

NOTES